S0-BSC-766

GALLANT AND LIBERTINE

For Renée Waldinger,
with best regards
Daniel Gerould

Gallant and Libertine

Eighteenth-Century French Divertissements and Parades

Edited, translated, and with an Introduction, by
Daniel Gerould

PERFORMING ARTS JOURNAL PUBLICATIONS
NEW YORK

GALLANT AND LIBERTINE

© 1983 Copyright by Performing Arts Journal Publications
Translation © 1983 by Daniel Gerould

First Edition
All rights reserved
No part of this publication may be reproduced or transmitted in any form or by any means, electronic or mechanical, including photocopy, recording, or any information storage or retrieval system now known or to be invented, without permission in writing from the publishers, except by a reviewer who wishes to quote brief passages in connection with a review written for inclusion in a magazine, newspaper, or broadcast.

Library of Congress Cataloging in Publication Data
Gallant and Libertine
Library of Congress Catalog Card No.: 83-61194
ISBN: 0-933826-48-6 (cloth)
ISBN: 0-933826-49-4 (paper)

All rights reserved under the International and Pan-American Copyright Conventions. For information, write to Performing Arts Journal Publications, 325 Spring Street, Room 318, New York, N.Y. 10013.

CAUTION: Professionals and amateurs are warned that the plays appearing herein are fully protected under the Copyright Laws of the United States and all other countries of the Copyright Union. All rights including professional, amateur, motion picture, recitation, lecturing, public readings, radio and television broadcasting, and the rights of translation into foreign languages, are strictly reserved. No performances or readings of these works may be given without the express authorization of the translator or his agent. For performance rights, contact Samuel French, 25 West 45th Street, New York, N.Y. 10036.

Design: Gautam Dasgupta
Printed in the United States of America

Publication of this book has been made possible in part by a grant from the National Endowment for the Arts, Washington, D.C., a federal agency, and public funds received from the New York State Council on the Arts.

PAJ Playscripts
General Editors: Bonnie Marranca and Gautam Dasgupta

Grateful acknowledgement is made to the following friends and colleagues who read the translations and offered helpful advice: Albert Bermel, Steven Hart, Catherine Morel, Jeanine Plottel, Robert Pucci, Mark Spergel and the Directors Collective, and Elizabeth Swain. — Daniel Gerould

Contents

Reprinted permission of Musée du Louvre

GILLES by Antoine Watteau

Eighteenth-Century French Divertissements and Parades

The ten plays that I have chosen for this collection—two one-act comedies by Marivaux and eight short parades, or farces, by Gueullette, Beaumarchais, and Potocki—are a holiday from the official and the orthodox. Unconventional works in minor genres reveal aspects of life and art in eighteenth-century France that the better known classics ignore. These irregular dramatic miniatures deal openly with sex and revel in human aggression and irrationality; they flout decency and decorum and embrace lazzi and improvisation; they celebrate the histrionic impulse to play. These little comedies and farces offer a picture of the Age of Reason that is far from reasonable. The world they portray is perverse, violent, and outrageous—in other words, like our own.

I propose a revision of the view that eighteenth-century French drama is tame and genteel. Littleness may be quintessential as well as cute, and theatre and art history, criticism, sociology, anthropology, and biography can be encapsulated in texts of the smallest proportions. These divertissements, gallants and libertine, take us to the heart of enlightenment concerns with sexism, racism, colonialism, reflections on travel, savages, and civilization, and obsessions with social class, masters and servants, power and revolution. Above all, they are expressions of a theatricalized conception of life.

AN ALTERNATIVE TRADITION:
FAIRGROUNDS AND COMMEDIA

By the eighteenth century the classic dramatic form that Corneille, Molière, and Racine had brought to perfection was exhausted. The old conventions seemed a dead weight, and the public was tired of masterpieces and the tyranny of literary texts. New life came from below—from the popular arts unbounded by neo-classical rules and regulations. Twin sources of inspiration were the fairgrounds and the Théâtre Italien with its Italian actors trained in *commedia dell'arte*. To give French drama fresh vigor, sophisticated artists turned to the naive amusements of the common people and to the Italian tradition of improvised outdoor entertainments using stock types and masks. (Another eighteenth-century French attempt at theatrical renewal, led by Diderot, went to British middle-class tragedy and fiction—Lillo's *The London Merchant* and Richardson's *Clarissa*—in the name of reality and social relevance, but except for theoretical treatises, this experiment in creating a serious bourgeois genre midway between tragedy and comedy did not bear any lasting fruit until the nineteenth century with Hebbel and Ibsen.)

The Italian comedians, expelled from France in 1697 by Louis XIV because of disrespectful references to Madame de Maintenon (secretly married to the King), had returned in 1716, and were celebrated for their natural style, freedom of gesture, and mastery of improvisation. For Marivaux, who presented many of his plays at the Théâtre Italien, the Italian company represented an alternative to the high formality of the Comédie Française, which insisted on regularity of subject and treatment and embalmed the plays that it produced in a declamatory style of acting.

The fairground theatres, offering low fare to suit plebeian tastes, fascinated the cultural elite. Well-to-do middle-class citizens, artists and intellectuals, and members of the aristocracy flocked to the fairs to enjoy the burlesques and parades, savor the ludicrous popular language in which they were written, and bring back new repertory for their own private theatres. The "society stages" in aristocratic chateaus and wealthy mansions permitted a freedom from decorum and the proprieties unthinkable at the Comédie Française and other establishment theatres. Nine of the ten plays in this collection—all except *The Dispute* which had one unsuccessful performance at the Comédie Française —were originally presented on society stages by amateur actors for select audiences.

SHORT FORMS AND MINOR GENRES

The fairgrounds, Théâtre Italien, and private theatres provided a refuge for the comic spirit at a time when the official drama was growing increasingly sentimental and didactic. Unorthodox short forms, such as Marivaux's one-acts and the parades by Gueullette, Beaumarchais, and Potocki, constituted an attack on classical regularity, which meant much ponderous scaffolding: rhymed verse, earnest moralizing, five acts of intricate plotting, with slow exposition and long-delayed recognitions leading to a tedious denouement that revealed to the spectators what they already knew.

Short forms in drama tend to be iconoclastic and innovative. They violate traditional expectations of established dramatic modes; they subvert the demands of ruling dogmas; they offer escape from reigning conventions and canons. Short forms start and stop abruptly. They avoid the architectonically predictable in favor of spontaneity and surprise. The microdramatist cuts through the circuitous unfoldings of full-scale playwriting into the bright, epigrammatic world of dreams, jokes, and aphorisms; he wields arbitrary bolts of theatrical suddenness. Short forms are *faits accomplis*. Instead of roundness and symmetry, they cultivate the elliptical. Too brief to be more than a fragment, an interrogation, a limited angle of vision, short forms do not uphold a structure or affirm a system.

In 1889 August Strindberg declared the short one-act play to be the best expression of modern sensibility and the drama of the future, even citing an eighteenth-century minor genre, the dramatic proverb, as a forerunner. The shorter the dramatic form, the more it rocks the pompous edifice of theatre and its hallowed traditions—as witness twentieth-century miniature nonsense plays by Achille Campanile, Ring Lardner, Konstanty Ildefons Gałczyński, and Jacques Prévert.

The eighteenth century excelled in small-scale art forms and showed a preference for miniaturization and reduction in dimensions. The offhand and impromptu were marks of style in a period that prized the conversational tone and had a passion for small objects. Many minor genres of drama flourished in the age of enlightenment, and unorthodox eighteenth-century short forms were as varied as Marivaux's elegant and philosophical one-act comedies and the boisterous and vulgar parades.

THE FÊTE GALANTE

Acting was the primordial art in the age of enlightenment; theatre inspired painting and provided it with much of its subject matter. In a minor genre of eighteenth-century painting known as the *fête galante*, Antoine Watteau —Marivaux's counterpart in the visual arts—depicts the social games, masquerades, and dances of elegant young couples who have left the artifice-bound salons for the fresh air of spacious parks and pavilions. In this bucolic world, the celebrants of the fête—wearing the fancy dress of *commedia* or elegant costumes from a past epoch—play their parts in a spontaneous pastoral drama, whereby the legend of the Golden Age is re-enacted. Rejecting rigid courtly forms, the artful revelers, enveloped in floral settings, flirt with a lost state of innocence and past simplicity, when man was in perfect harmony with nature.

The garden of earthly paradise becomes a theatricalized entertainment in which the first dwellers are *commedia* characters. The atavistic vision of a departed world implies what Diderot calls "a secret wish to escape deep into the forest, a call to return to the primal dwelling place." With its magical countryside where carefree lovers are always happy, the *fête galante* is a nostalgic spectacle, expressive of the eighteenth-century Arcadian ideal of fusing natural and artificial man in such a way as to provide liberation from the fetters of civilization while retaining all its advantages. But unreconcilable tensions between instinct and morality impart to Watteau's gallant paintings an underlying tone of melancholy. The gap between the idyllic world of unrestrained erotic fulfillment and the civilized world of ethical culture can be bridged only by play.

THE PURSUIT OF PLEASURE

The *fête galante* reflects a society dedicated to the pursuit of pleasure. Enjoyment is the only goal of a self-absorbed leisure class that lives surrounded by mirrors. Contemplation of the self and its desires becomes the principal amusement. "Pleasure," according to the enlightenment philosopher Claude-Adrien Helvétius, is "the soul of the universe." Without believing in the artificial forms of polite society, the jaded players accept the conventions simply as the rules of the game, designed to enhance the pleasures of sexual conquest. Living moment by moment results in the miniaturization of time; each instant must be seized and savored for itself. The impermanence of atomized feelings leads to superficial contacts, casual love-making, constant change of partners, and betrayal by mutual consent. Egotism, narcissism, hedonism make infidelity pandemic. In Montesquieu's *Persian Letters*, one of the Persian travelers visiting Paris observes:

> The French do not admire constancy much. They believe it is as ridiculous to swear abiding love to one woman as it is to maintain that they will forever be in good health, or invariably happy. When they promise always to love a woman, they suppose that she, in turn, promises that she will always be lovable; if she breaks her word, they no longer feel bound to theirs.

Diderot, in the *Supplement to Bougainville's "Voyage,"* has his polygamous Tahitian native Orou tell the horrifed European Chaplain that constancy is contrary to the laws of nature.

> Can you, in fact, think of anything more senseless than a precept that proscribes the perpetual change that is within us, that orders us to

show a constancy not in our nature, and that violates the natures and the liberties of both male and female by chaining them to each other for their whole lives? Can you think of anything more senseless than a fidelity that limits the most capricious of all our pleasures to a single object, than a vow of immutability taken by two beings made of flesh in the sight of a sky that does not remain the same for a single instant?

In Crébillon fils's *The Night and the Moment*, the libertine hero explains that men and women in past ages felt obliged to be virtuous or at least appear so because of old-fashioned moral prejudices. Now that modern philosophy has swept away these foolish bugbears, enlightened human beings can pursue their own self-gratification.

Never have women been less hypocritical in society; never has there been less affectation of virtue. Two people appeal to each other; they do not deny themselves pleasure. Do they grow tired of one another? They part with just as little ceremony as when they coupled. Do they appeal to each other a second time? They start all over again with as much enthusiasm as if it were the first time that they were together. They part once more, but never do they quarrel. It is true that love has nothing whatsover to do with any of this; but what is love but a desire, whose importance has been exaggerated, an agitation of the senses, which human vanity has elevated to the rank of a virtue. To-day we know that only inclination exists; and if we still make professions of love, it is less because we believe it than because it is the most civilized fashion of asking our partner for what we feel a need.

Marivaux's *The Dispute* will have much to say on the topic of inconstancy.

CULTURE AS PLAY

Members of the upper-class in the age of enlightenment filled their leisure with games and play: carnivals, balls, festivities, divertissements, cards and gaming. It was, in the words of the Goncourt brothers, a dancing century. In *Homo Ludens: A Study of the Play Element in Culture*, Johan Huizinga singles out the eighteenth century as a period in which culture itself was "played." Present not only in pastimes and entertainments, the play element pervades such diverse activities as conversation, love, and art. Seen in this light, libertinage and promiscuity become dramatic games with intricate dance-like movements. Art, allied to fashion and style, does not imitate nature, but is free to create an autonomous world of play.

In an age dedicated to amusement not only is the theatre a metaphor for life, but life itself is highly theatricalized. The theatricalized self—self-seeking, self-serving, self-scrutinizing—is always in quest of an audience. The passion for playacting exists at the highest levels of society, where every aristocratic residence has its own stage. But the concept of "private theatre" extends beyond the actual playhouses built for the wealthy and well-born to all those situations in social life where freedom from constraint can be found in impersonation, or where titillating shows can be witnessed by indiscreet peeking.

The impromptu peepshow is a specialty of eighteenth-century erotic play-culture. Oglers and voyeurs are plentiful in novels, plays, and the visual arts. The furtive glance is a recurrent motif in the painting of the period. Fragonard's famous "The Lucky Hazards of the Swing" shows a gallant so skillfully positioned in the shrubbery that he can look up the skirts of the swinging lady, and in many licentious engravings leering gentlemen peer through keyholes and windows or lurk behind curtains and spy on fleshy ladies as they bathe, disrobe, climb in and out of bed, or are given enemas by their maids.

Marivaux's conception of man and of life in society is intensely theatrical, and covert watchers are key figures in his comedies, manipulating the action and staging plays within plays. Because of their heightened awareness, these hidden spectators control the game and are the masters, watching every move made by their puppets and slaves with an omniscient and omnipresent eye.

TRAVELERS' TALES AND THE MYTH OF ORIGINS

Eighteenth-century travels to exotic countries, voyages of exploration to the New World and to the Orient, and discoveries of savage lands and primitive tribes led to curiosity about the origins of humankind and to reconstructions of the myth of the Golden Age, Eden, and "First Times." Civilized man felt the need to rediscover the sources of his culture, to view his own past in historical perspective, and to understand himself and his present position by retracing his steps.

Unable to go beyond a Eurocentric colonial ideology that took its own achievements as the absolute measure, the age of enlightenment saw the primitive state of man, reflected in the savage world of Indians, aborigines, Tahitians, as an early stage on the way to civilization and a necessary passage from infancy to maturity. And yet at the same time the opposition between nature and culture, innocence and civilization, central to eighteenth-century philosophy, enabled enlightenment writers and thinkers to contrast the vices of a corrupt world already in its old age and decline with the natural virtues of primitive man. Through imaginative or experimental means, attempts were made to go back to the beginnings of time and there discover the natural laws that existed in the primeval state, by which the artificial and morally degenerate standards of civilized societies could be judged.

Travelers' tales gave rise to an awareness of the parochial nature of the supposedly absolute Christian precepts about sex, marriage, and the position of women. Cultural relativism grew with the recognition of many other systems of belief and of a wide spectrum of contrasting manners and morals. As the old certainties crumbled, neither man's nature nor woman's place seemed immutably fixed. Codes of sexual conduct became a crucial test case, since monogamous marriage, with its ideal of fidelity, raised disturbing questions about the ability of religion and society to impose artificial rules on recalcitrant nature.

Islands play an important role in eighteenth-century French comedy. The idea of transporting civilized Europeans to a far-off isle peopled by savages was first used in fairground performances for its exotic, comic, and spectacular possibilities. Then, in 1721, Delisle's *Savage Harlequin*, in which the freedom of a savage is contrasted with the tyranny of masters over slaves in a civilized world of riches and power, enjoyed great success at the Théâtre Italien and established the vogue of the island play. By transposition to an imaginary isle, topical social subjects and controversial philosophical themes could be distanced and made to appear less subversive, while through the confrontation of two different worlds, oblique yet pointed criticism could be made of the reigning culture. (It is interesting to note that Soviet playwrights would find a similar use for island plays in the 1920s and '30s.)

MODERN MARIVAUX

Marivaux's comedies are considerably less sunny, gentle, and optimistic than we have been led to believe. The awakening of love, Marivaux's preferred theme, is by no means innocent, since the discovery of self, which it entails, brings an awareness of power over others and the ability and need to dominate—and to hurt. Like most comic writers, Marivaux has a gloomy view of human nature. Nowhere is this more apparent than in *The Dispute* and *The Colony*, which reveal the author at his most disabused. *The Dispute* shows us a fallen world in the making, where vanity and promiscuity hold sway. Love is an irrational force of nature which its victims cannot understand, much less control. In *The Colony* society consists of warring factions that are unable to reform and constitute a harmonious whole; instead, class and sexual conflicts are extended to encompass national and imperialistic warfare.

In his relentless analysis of the hostile relations between the sexes and the social classes, Marivaux discloses who wields power over whom, out of what demands of the ego the need for conquest arises, and through which signs and symbols domination is asserted. Two stages can be discerned: the first, in *The Dispute*, the awakening of self as an individual, or sexual identity in adolescence, resulting in capricious pairings-off and the instability of couples; and second, in *The Colony*, the awakening of self as a member of a larger group, or gender identity in women, causing conflict within already formed pairs and among classes.

THE DISPUTE

Marivaux's most metaphysical drama, *The Dispute* is an inquest into the origins of infidelity, an attempt to locate the fatal flaw in the human heart that threatens the stability of the world. By means of an experiment, the seeds of the almost universal inconstancy of present times can be discovered in the lost Golden Age. The *tabula rasa* to which mankind is returned quickly generates the same vices and betrayals that plague civilization. The most primitive stage in the development of the world and the old age of human society are linked by the permanence in man of jealousy and vanity and the pleasure he derives from feeling superior to others.

But, we may ask, following the principles of modern science, does not the framing of the experiment influence its outcome? The observers and their observing are crucial elements in the demonstration. The watching experimenters, divided among themselves along gender lines, and each seeking to place the blame on the opposite sex, hope to justify their own infidelities and betrayals by insuring that their guinea pigs fail the test of constancy.

What is the spatial structure of *The Dispute*? A series of complex refractions. Watched by the audience hidden in the auditorium, the Prince and his entourage, hidden in the theatre, watch two young couples watched by two black servants. And what do all these watchers see? The young couples watching themselves and one another as they discover their own images reflected in stream, mirror, portrait, and eyes. Love is a form of self-contemplation that insists on being shared by admiring contemplators.

In Marivaux's Edenic replay, the creation of man becomes a *fête galante* for the Prince and his courtiers. Peeping from behind high walls (used to pen the young couples in like animals) into a regimented earthly paradise, ruled over by black guardian angels, aging representatives of a decayed culture witness the awakening of the first man and woman. Replacing the fruit of the tree of knowledge, a mirror causes the Fall. Self is the serpent.

The harmony of nature and civilization has gone awry in the wild overgrown garden. Civilization—all deceit, subterfuge, manipulation—is degenerate; nature—all cruel egotism—is ready for corruption. Love is only self-affirmation in which the narcissistic "I" seeks new verifications in an endless round of experiences.

The Dispute is rich in associations with the Near East, tales of origin, the pastoral. In Book II of Herodotus's *Histories* there is the story of King Psammetichus of Egypt who conducted an experiment to discover if the Egyptians were the most ancient of all races; he took two new born twins and had them brought up in isolation in order to learn what language they would speak and thus establish the ur-tongue of the world. The Prince is like a potentate from *The Arabian Nights Entertainment*. Adam and Eve have become Azor and Egle in a new genesis. *Egle* is the name of a sixteenth-century novella and pastoral tragicomedy by Giraldi Cinthio.

Unconventional in theme and technique, *The Dispute* was too disturbing a work to be understood or accepted in its own time. The text abounds in ambiguities. Is the Prince mistaken in asserting that his two black assistants are brother and sister? Carisse and Mesrou themselves imply that they are lovers, or husband and wife. Is their relationship incestuous, because they have lived in isolation with their wards for almost two decades, denied any other choice of mate? Is this the natural state of man? Or are the blacks only pretending to be lovers in order to manipulate their young charges when they claim that frequent separations alone can sustain passion? And is this counsel given sincerely or in full knowledge that it will produce the opposite effect?

As the blacks subtly contrive and control the moves of the two amorous couples, are they acting according to the Prince's wishes, or their own secret desires? And are Carisse and Mesrou working in concert or at cross purposes in a gender war, each striving to prove the opposite sex faithless? Which are the strongest loyalties: among members of the same social class, among members of the same sex, between masters and their servants? The black servants are masters of their white pupils but servants of their white masters. They are intermediaries between the experimenters and the guinea pigs, sharing characteristics of each.

The awakening of the self and its desires not only produces inconstancy in matters of the heart, it also constitutes a threat to authority and the reigning hierarchy. When the blacks attempt to re-assert their dominion with the reminder, "We're your masters," one of the headstrong lovers, resentful of any constraint, replies, "My masters? What's a master?" Efforts to suppress instinct seem a form of tyranny to the young; rebellion is in the air.

The most startling theatrical element in *The Dispute*, the two blacks, are reflections of eighteenth-century concerns with race that are social, aesthetic, and moral. Ever since Peter the Great adorned the Russian court with his Abyssinian Negro favorite Hannibal (grandfather of the poet Alexander Pushkin), all the great families of Eastern Europe felt obliged to display colored retainers. In paintings, graphics, and fashion designs of the period (including the *fête galante*), black pages serve as contrasts to set off the white skin of the lords and ladies, often holding parasols to protect their masters and mistresses from the sun and any possibility of tanning, then regarded as ugly. For philosophers and social critics, the enslavement of the African by the European represented natural man's loss of freedom and dignity in the name of a supposedly higher order of culture.

Ironically, the black victims in *The Dispute* are required to enforce the discontents of civilization on other unwilling objects of oppression, extending the chain of domination downwards. The young couples experimented on are obviously from the lower classes, the children of servants, since only poor parents would permit their offspring to be taken from them for such a cruel purpose in return for payment. But there is no solidarity among the oppress- ed. The young lovers are ethnocentric as well as egocentric, finding black features unattractive and showing no tolerance for human beings made in an image other than their own. The colonial attitudes of the Prince and his court are reflected in their poor subjects.

The play seems about to end as the Prince and his retinue re-enter and the two faithless couples for the first time see themselves through the civilized eyes of their god-like judges; they perceive their own nakedness and shame prior to being expelled from the garden. At this point a surprise: the unexpected ar- rival of a third pair of lovers personifying a fidelity so rare that it arouses ad- miration in the jaded Prince and his companion Hermiane who declare they will assure the financial security of such an exemplary couple—further evidence of the plebeian origins of the guinea pigs. Earlier the Prince had disclosed the existence of only two pairs of young people. The *coup de théâtre* of the unexplained third pair gives the illusion of an affirmative denouement. But troublesome questions remain. After the convincing demonstration of the inconstancy of the human heart, ruled by vanity, pride, and self-interest, do the noble sentiments of the third pair suggest the possibility of enduring love in the face of overwhelming odds? Are they the exception that proves the rule? Or is their belief in inconstancy what Diderot calls "the vain delusion enter- tained by two children who know nothing about themselves and who are blinded by a momentary ecstasy to the mutability of all that is around them"? In any case, they will be well paid for being virtuous and get a pension for upholding an idealistic code that a cynical society professes to esteem, but never practices. Could these smug lovers unwittingly be the worst lackeys of a hypocritical system?

With its multi-layers of spectators/performance and its resources of silence, gesture, object, *The Dispute* is a departure from purely verbal theatre, inviting director and actors to explore a range of unstated emotions and attitudes; the text is polysemic, raising questions to which no answers can be found and opening vistas on the future. No wonder two powerful creative forces in con- temporary theatre, Patrice Chéreau in France, and Henryk Tomaszewski in Poland, have been drawn to this enigmatic work and sought to reveal its hid- den depths. Expanding the play to full length through the addition of a pro- logue based on Marivaux's reflective essays, Chéreau in his three stagings (1973-1976) transforms *The Dispute* into a ritual drama of initiation into the mysteries of the universe. Aided by his two black shamanistic healers, the Prince forces his aging lady love and her court to confront their spiritual sickness. Eros turns the four young lovers into wild beasts, and the high walls of the castle whirl about, driving the young couples apart and finally assuming the shape of an urban metropolis. In his production at the Wrocław Mime Company in 1979, Tomaszewski, dispensing with words altogether, indicts the decadent Prince and his court by a detailed portrayal of their orgies. After staging a play by Lope de Vega, the bored, debauched courtiers spy upon the naked young lovers happy in their innocence. The Prince seduces and corrupts the trusting heroine, who leaves behind her nakedness for an elegant court costume. In a closing diminuendo, the Prince, who has defeated Hermiane in the dispute, is left alone with an ironic smile on his face. After his departure, there remain on the empty stage only the two black servants, symbols of violated nature. Tools of a cynical master, they themselves have violated youth with their white-gloved hands, now raised aloft like totems.

THE COLONY

Here the *fête galante* turns to sexual politics. *The Colony* presents an attempted reconstruction of society in the name of equality between the sexes, not by going back to the paradise lost of "First Times" (as in *The Dispute*), but through a geopolitical transposition to an exotic savage isle. But the utopian experiment in making the world over by restoring natural rights in a garden setting and undoing the flaws of civilization fails because of the re-assertion of the old divisive rivalries and pride of power. Community fragments into hostile groups of gender and class, who join together only to oppress an even more "alien" group, the island's natives.

No longer willing to be servants of male masters, the women of *The Colony* demythify the idea of supposedly innate feminine roles by distinguishing between nature and nurture. But they overlook the fact that liberation of women cannot be achieved until equality of classes and races is also established. *The Colony* is an abortive feminist drama placed in the larger context of class and colonial conflict.

Marivaux wrote three utopian island comedies—*The Isle of Slaves, The Isle of Reason*, and *The Colony*—in which he explores through zero situations the origin and nature of inequalities between masters and servants, men and women, and members of different social classes. Drawing upon Aristophanes's *Women's Congress* for the idea of a feminist revolt, Marivaux in *The Colony* introduces the destructive germ of civilization into an idyllic natural setting—the place of action resembles an eighteenth-century French colony on the Mississippi. An early three-act version, *The New Colony, or The League of Women*, had been withdrawn by Marivaux after one disastrous performance at the Théâtre Italien in 1729. Revised as a one-act play and given a private performance by amateurs in 1750 on a society stage, *The Colony*, although published the same year, was not included in Marivaux's collected works until 1878 and not seen again in the theatre until the mid-twentieth century. It remained too unconventional and forward-looking for two centuries.

European civilization, as brought to the island by the colonists, maintains itself by the dynamics of warfare. The structure of *The Colony* is defined by four wars; the first and the last, framing the play, are external conflicts, the middle pair internal or civil struggles. National war with a victorious European enemy has made the losers exiles and driven them to the island as a refuge. War between the sexes soon breaks out and leads to a feminist rebellion. Class warfare between the aristocratic and working-class leadership destroys the unity of the women's revolt. Finally, trumped-up colonial war against an imagined enemy, the indigenous savages, is used to divert the women from their cause and, in an atmosphere of manipulated crisis, once again make them submissive to male authority. One war replaces another, as successive outlets for feelings of aggression and frustration must be found.

The women engage in conflict as defined by the men; they wish to be equally bellicose and wage their polemical battles in military style, with trumpet and drum, rallies and proclamations. The struggle becomes a matter of costume and appearance, and invective centers around hats and headdress, the signs and symbols of professions from which the women are excluded. By trying to play the men's contentious games and wield masculine weapons, the women are ultimately beaten when challenged to bear arms and lead the troops in the defense of the colony.

Class structure determines the play's mechanism. At the top of the social hierarchy in *The Colony* are the aristocrats, Arthenice (her name an anagram of Catherine, the Marquise de Rambouillet, famous *précieuse* of the preceding century) and Lord Timagenes; at the bottom are the commoners, the artisan Sorbin and his wife. In between are two members of a middle class, Persinet and Hermocrates, who hope to profit from their position as observers of the gender conflict. Persinet, an educated commoner who has reached a high level of refinement and delicacy (in the earlier three-act version the subtle Harlequin had this role), is too much in love with Madam Sorbin's daughter to have any detachment or ability to maneuver.

Hermocrates (the name comes from Hermes, messenger of the gods) is the true intermediary—the covert watcher or voyeur-manipulator who pulls the strings and controls the action, successfully sabotaging the women's revolution and preserving the status quo. Both his position within the hierarchy and his role within the comedy are slippery.

Hermocrates is allied by sensibility and style to the aristocracy, from whom he is indistinguishable in manners and dress. He represents the emergent upper bourgeois class placed between the nobility, who have adopted him as one of their own, and the proletariat, with whom he will soon form a temporary political alliance to advance his own notions of freedom and power. Although his first indicated appearance comes more than halfway through the play, I believe that in production Hermocrates should be shown as present from the start, watching both sides, seizing upon human weakness, and penetrating through high-flown rhetoric to the ruling motives of vanity, pride, and self-interest. Distanced from all camps, and emotionally uninvolved, he is in a position to serve as chief political mover and power broker between groups.

Here Marivaux forecasts the role of the upper bourgeoisie in the Revolution. Identified with the nobility as part of the ruling cultural elite, the middle class uses the lower classes to effect the Revolution and gain new political liberties and powers, after which it abandons its working-class allies. The bourgeois intellectual Hermocrates is taken for one of the aristocracy until the crucial moment when Madam Sorbin, the puritanical working-class revolutionary, in a surprising *coup de théâtre*, proclaims her plan for abolishing the nobility. At this point Hermocrates reveals his bourgeois origins and claims ideological unity with the working-class—but he makes these disclosures only to subvert the women's revolution for middle-class goals. The liberal philosopher—a master of the compromise and the sell-out—prevents the men from capitulating to the women's demands and preserves the existing system of male authority, with only the promise of a few paternalistic concessions to be made to the women later on.

Despite his proclaimed allegiance to democracy, Hermocrates exploits class antagonisms among the women, which prove stronger than their unity on the basis of gender. It is easy to split Arthenice and Madam Sorbin, two women who are opposed in all matters—class, temperament, attitudes on sexual morality—except feminist aspirations. By arousing vanity, jealousy, and pride, the bourgeois philosopher first divides the opposition; then by staging a bogus colonial war against absent and non-belligerent natives, he reaffirms the women's passivity and dependence on the men.

The characters who serve as an implicit measure of the Europeans and their civilization—the savages—are never shown by Marivaux. I would propose a theatrical reading of *The Colony* in which a pair of savages, constantly on stage hidden in a grove, watch the Europeans—a gentle, peaceful couple, young lovers, naked, unwarlike, living harmoniously in nature. Thus would innocence spy upon experience (reversing the situation in *The Dispute*), and the incomprehension of the natives and their lack of any manipulative drive for power and control would be their most telling commentary.

The seeming conventionality of the sudden ending to *The Colony* is only apparent. Reasons for the collapse of the revolt are astutely drawn and ironically dramatized. The denouement shows how class antagonisms can be used to undermine feminine solidarity. The women are diverted from their real enemy—authoritarian men and an unjust social structure—and set against one another and other victims of oppression. Class pride, ethnocentricity, patriotism prove more tenacious than gender loyalties. A colonial war is used to quell possible internal revolt. Imperialistic jingoism is the bulwark of male chauvinism.

Because it does not become a genuine social revolution, the women's rebellion is easily subverted. The women seek freedom from enslavement —unattainable at home—in the colony, but fail to perceive that their gains will be at the expense of the natives who must inevitably be enslaved. It does not occur to the women, who wish to share what they metaphorically call "the farm" with the men, that this farm actually belongs to the savages and that any sharing must first of all be with the indigenous population. The hope for a perfected social order based on principles of equality comes to naught; the very notion of civilization seems to imply warring factions, self-interest, and the drive for power.

WHAT IS A PARADE: HISTORY AND ORIGINS

A type of farce with characters derived from *commedia*, the parade flourished in early eighteenth-century France as a popular fairground entertainment presented gratis on a raised platform or balcony outside the theatre and designed to entice spectators to pay to see the show inside. Its origins lay in burlesque scenes presented by clowns and acrobats in front of the Hôtel de Bourgogne and at the fairs at Saint Germain and Saint Laurent towards the end of the sixteenth century.

Purveying low buffoonery geared to the taste of the common people, the parade quickly became a craze with the upper classes who flocked to the fairgrounds and attempted to master its vulgar language and slapstick style. Lively interchange took place between the robust popular arts and elite high culture; Marie Antoinette and her court ladies took lessons with fishwives in order to learn to speak billingsgate. Soon the repertory of the fairs was adopted by the society stages and private theatres, and well-known writers began composing literary parades for special performances. The primitive outdoor sideshow with its mountebank's come-on (skillfully evoked in Beaumarchais's *Seven League Boots*) was transformed into a sophisticated theatrical form, a pseudo-popular genre, that artfully simulated the crude naiveté of a fairground entertainment.

In the entry on the parade in Diderot's *Encyclopedia* (1765), the components of the genre are given as its popular roots, fashionable standing, low humor, and four recurring stereotyped characters. Elderly Cassander, a descendant of the *commedia*'s Pantalone, is the quintessential bourgeois who plays the role of father, tutor, senile suitor, or aged libertine. Charming Isabelle, like her witty, strong-minded Italian namesake, is a high-spirited young girl of questionable virginity and outspoken views who dominates both father and lovers. The handsome Leander, son of a rabbit skin dealer or candle-snuffer at the Comédie Française, is no more than a corporal in the reserves but passes himself off as an elegant dandy and fire-breathing dragon. The doltish but appealing valet Giles, descended from Pedrolino or Pierrot in the *commedia*, is sometimes paired off against the more adroit and roguish Harlequin.

Popular art forms thrive on seemingly fixed and repetitive formulas. A typical parade shows the widower Cassander who must make a business trip to the Indies, Persia, or America instructing his blockheaded servant Giles to guard his sixteen-year-old daughter Isabelle from the marauding Leander. Eight months pregnant, already delivered of two or three children, Isabelle vows to enter a convent rather than give up her heart's desire. After beatings and kickings, collisions and pile-ups, trickery and disguises, the foreordained denouement, known to every spectator, comes abruptly: Isabelle and Leander kneel at Cassander's feet and obtain his permission to marry. As in the comic strips, out of the apparently limited opportunities offered by this restricted cast of characters and situations, an endless number of variations are worked by the authors of the parades. Much of the enjoyment for the audience lay in recognition of familiar characters going through their traditional paces.

Unlike *commedia dell'arte* scenarios, the texts of the parades contain fully written out dialogue, but in the stage directions scope is left the actors for improvisation and the creation of *lazzi* and gags. The language of the parades, as stylized and artificial as its characters and plots, is a riotous jumble of obscenity, error, and illogic. Normal speech is deformed by mispronunciations, grammatical blunders, malapropisms, and indecent double meanings. Because of faulty *liaison* or word-linkage in French, Isabelle becomes Zisabelle, Zirzabelle, or Zerzabelle; Leander is distorted as Liander. Sometimes all these linguistic malformations were fully written out in the text, sometimes not (alternate versions exist of some of the plays)—but the actors always spoke the parade dialect, a special creation like the language of our comic strips and animated cartoons.

Unbridled verbal fantasy is a major weapon of comedy. With its outrageous titles, absurd stories, erotic and scatological jokes about virginity, pregnancy, bodily parts and functions, the often gross and always irreverent parades violate the taboos of polite conversation and behavior, and parody the tearful recognitions, pious kneelings, and heartfelt sentiments of serious eighteenth-century comedy (from which the comic had been banished).

Introduced into the great chateaus as a society divertissement and performed by the aristocratic hosts and their guests, the parades enjoyed a vogue on the private stages of the nobility that lasted from the 1730s until the time of the Revolution. Famous professional actors from Paris—breaking the rules of their contracts and risking heavy fines—were often hired to appear in what amounted to clandestine performances. A number of celebrated authors essayed the genre, including Voltaire and Nivelle de la Chaussée (best known for his *comédies-larmoyantes* or weeping comedies).

The three outstanding practitioners of the eighteenth-century parade—at the beginning, middle, and end of the period—were Gueullette, Beaumarchais, and Potocki. These multi-talented authors not only wrote, staged, and acted in their own parades, but they also engaged in a variety of literary and paraliterary activities and played colorful and often dramatic roles in the public life of their times. Their love of the parades was more than a youthful abberation ("*delicta juventutis meae* or sins of my youth" was Gueullette's formulation); it expressed their commitment to life theatricalized and culture as play.

GUEULLETTE: CRIMINOLOGY AND FARCE

Thomas Simon Gueullette (1683-1776) was the creator of the literary parade and its most enthusiastic proponent. He edited the three-volume *Théâtre des Boulevards*, published anonymously in 1756, and was himself the author of most, if not all, the twenty-six parades contained in the collection. His name—*gueule* is colloquial French for face or mug—boded well for a writer of farce.

From an old bourgeois family, Gueullette made a successful career as a lawyer and legal scholar, becoming assistant public prosecutor while still in his twenties. He led the orderly life of a model citizen and public servant. During working hours he methodically tracked down wrong-doers and kept extensive annotated files on atrocious crimes and punishments, including his own eyewitness account of the hideous execution of Damiens (used in Peter Weiss's *Marat/Sade*)—the would-be assassin of Louis XV who was tortured to death for an hour and a half by sixteen executioners—and featuring gruesome details about murders, poisonings, rapes, seductions, kidnappings, and broken marriages due to sexual malformation, impotence, and adultery.

In his spare time Gueullette led another life, entirely devoted to jollity and comedy, as novelist, playwright, translator, theatre historian, and editor. The public prosecutor was the author of dozens of volumes of fairy tales and exotic stories, popularizing the genre of the Oriental tale with his *Tartar Tales*, *Chinese Tales*, and *Mogul Tales*. From the Italian he translated works such as *The Decameron*, and he edited many French classics, including Montaigne and Rabelais.

The theatre was Gueullette's life-long avocation. At the age of eleven he went to see a performance by the Italian actors and later became their friend and supporter, writing many plays for the Italian company and helping members of the troupe with legal matters. A jovial man dedicated to the enjoyment of life, whose motto—taken from Horace—was *Dulce est desipere in loco* ("It is delightful to play the fool occasionally"), Gueullette refused to take money for his plays and gave the author's royalties to the actors. As theatre scholar, the public prosecutor collected *commedia* scenarios, wrote a history of the Italian theatre in France, and explored the origins of the parade, tracing its sources back to the Atelline farces and Greek prologues.

In 1707 Gueullette, then an apprentice lawyer, went with a group of his friends to the Saint Laurent fair, where they saw the parade, *Fortunatus's Hat* (in which Giles is sold the invisible hat trick), which so delighted the young attorneys that they went home and staged it themselves. Soon Gueullette and his fellow lawyers formed an amateur company. At first their theatre was in the house of the King's dancing master, Favier, whose son Jean was one of the actors and a close friend of Gueullette's. Gueullette played Harlequin, and between the acts the entire cast danced ballets composed by Favier. Their festive parades attracted high society from the court of Louis XV; performances started at eleven in the evening so that lords and ladies from Versailles could come after attending the "King's supper." Following the Venetian custom, masked guests were admitted and a ball took place after the plays.

Before long Gueullette was writing his own parades and staging them in his country house a few miles from Paris. Taking only the basic situation from the traditional scenarios, he created original dialogue and incidents. Fairground theatre managers now asked the public prosecutor to let them perform his parades at the fairs—an instructive case of popular art's readiness to adopt the high culture version of popular art. Gueullette's parades also traveled to distant points in Europe. His old friend Jean Favier, who had become ballet master to the King of Poland, took a number of the short plays to the Polish court where they were well received by the royal family.

Watteau's famous painting *Gilles* is a poster for one of Gueullette's longer parades in four parts, *The Education of Giles, or In Washing a Donkey's Head One Loses One's Soap*, in which Giles inherits money, obtains permission to marry Isabelle, but fails completely to pass a special course in culture and manners and loses both fortune and bride. In addition to the full-length portrait of Giles (to which I shall return), the painting shows from left to right, Cassander on the donkey, Isabelle, Leander wearing the coxcomb, and the master who has been attempting to educate Giles.

Guellette's parades were rediscovered in the twentieth century as direct links to *commedia dell'arte* and the great tradition of acting farce that had been all but lost in the age of realism. They were staged by Gaston Baty at the Studio des Champs-Élysées in 1924, by Jacques Copeau and his young disciples, the Copiaux, in 1925, and by the Comédiens Routiers in 1933, where they proved to be invaluable training for young actors.

Besides pure theatricality, Gueullette's parades contain satiric bite. In the cynical—and sometimes macabre and sadistic—joy that the author takes in portraying a world of swindlers and fools we can detect, I think, the professional stance of the public prosecutor exposing wrong-doing and fraud. Criminology and farce are not unrelated disciplines, and the dossiers of curious facts about human depravity that the legal scholar maintained served the comic author well in his double career as prosecutor and paradist.

In *The Blind One-Armed Deaf Mute* Gueullette creates comedy out of Giles's unwilling and suspicious compassion for someone worse off than he is—a totally dispossessed victim of society. Feigning progressive dismemberment and loss of his five senses, the Sharper mimes the plight of the incapacitated: the blind beggar, the workman injured on the job, the crippled soldier —discards of society, refuse littering the streets. Through absurd impersonations of the disabled, the Sharper tries to take advantage of Giles's good heart and stupidity. But in the battle with his generous impulses, Giles's self-interest always wins out. Although Giles's fundamental common sense proves no match for the Sharper's nonsense, there is a basis of folk wisdom in Giles's preference for money over sentiment. The tough fiber of the preposterous exchanges between the swindler and his dupe calls to mind another more extreme dismemberment farce, the clown act in Brecht's *Baden-Baden Learning Play*.

The Shit Merchant deals with another kind of refuse with which the streets in Paris and the Provinces were afloat during the eighteenth century. Like the *commedia*, the parades are often scatological, but the scatology in Gueullette's farce is more social and economic than physiological. Gueullette is less concerned with where human excrement comes from than with where it goes; problems of sanitation and waste disposal are at the bottom of the joke. What is underfoot everywhere is the subtext of *The Shit Merchant*. We know from Fernand Braudel's *Capitalism and Material Life 1400-1800* that eighteenth-century Paris stank from unemptied cesspools, that chamber pots were emptied out windows, that streets served as sewers, and that people relieved themselves publicly in corridors of buildings like the Louvre, under trees in the Tuileries, and along the banks of the Seine. The farce is economic in that Giles is without a profession, unemployed and unemployable, reduced to selling his own shit—a commodity with which, alas, the market is flooded.

In *The Two Doubles, or The Surprising Surprise*—a rare Giles-less but not guileless parade—Gueullette creates a psychodrama about the power of sexual fantasy and game playing to revitalize a sour marriage. Impotent old Cassander and his frigid young wife Isabelle stage a parade within a parade by acting the roles of handsome rake Leander and depraved whore Floozie. Through impersonation they find rejuvenation and liberation of their hidden desires. The theatricalization of life enables the discontented couple to discover second, opposing selves or doubles within their personalities and to overcome their inhibitions and frustrations. By means of *commedia* therapy, the pleasures of adultery without the risks become a corrective to the boredom of marriage.

The twice tautological title of *The Two Doubles, or the Surprising Surprise* illustrates the penchant of the parade for redundancy. Doubling—a venerable device of farce going back to Greek and Roman times—is a trademark of the genre. Giles himself is a double of the now more familiar Pierrot. First the *commedia* figure of Pierrot was assimilated by Giles in the early 1700s and then Giles was replaced by Pierrot one hundred years later. Such are the metamorphoses of one of the most popular and enduring comic masks.

GILES

The true star of the parade—and its most distinctive character—is Giles, a twin of Pierrot and always identically dressed in loose white clothes, long sleeves and ruff, with a flour-whitened face. More than a stock comic butt, Giles is a contradictory character able to elicit diverse responses. He is both selfish, greedy, and gluttonous, and also poetic, sensitive, and enchanting. He is a type frequently encountered in eighteenth-century French literature: the naive hero of child-like innocence to whom a series of adventures and misfortunes occur, as is the case with Voltaire's Candide and Lesage's Gil Blas.

The Giles of the fairgrounds—"he who runs away when called"—has been labeled a stupid, fearful lout, pushed around by others and unsuccessful in everything he undertakes. Primarily interested in food and sleeping, this coarse buffoon is the object of Leander's abuse and of Harlequin's practical joking and superior wit. Yet the Giles of the literary parades is always jolly and good-humored, sometimes sly and cunning, often wiser in his stupidity than the others in their cleverness. In Watteau's *Gilles,* in which a life-size figure of the white-face clown stands detached from his *commedia* cronies in a radiant natural setting, the hero of the parades acquires an introspective dimension. As painted by Watteau, Giles has been found—by various interpreters—to be likable but strange; shy, lonely, and gentle; aloof and sincere; awkward, absurd, yet touching.

Like all enduring creations of popular art, Giles has an enigmatic appeal that defies explanation. He can undergo multiple transformations. Permutation of roles is favored within the framework of the parade; playfulness, promiscuity, and mutability are keynotes of the genre. The stereotypical mask characters are eternally themselves, yet always different in their varied theatrical manifestations. Usually Cassander's valet, Giles is sometimes Leander's servant; occasionally he is Cassander's chief clerk, Isabelle's godfather, or even Cassander's friend sought after as a son-in-law. In one parade Giles is revealed to be Isabelle's father; in another he imagines that she loves him and asks for her hand in marriage; in yet another he has an attractive wife Gillette whom he successfully defends against attempted seductions.

Giles likewise has the ability to appeal to different audiences at different times and places. In the latter half of the eighteenth century he moved to the official public theatres and delighted Boulevard audiences, gaining admission to the stage of the Comédie-Italienne in 1767. Even after the *fête galantes* had been scattered by the Revolution, the super-plebeian Giles survived and drew crowds to small theatres such as the Funambules where, known by his alternate name of Pierrot, the white-faced clown gained new life in the pantomimes and harlequinades of Jean Gaspard Deburau. As interpreted by Deburau—a favorite of artists and poets—Giles-Pierrot grew melancholy, tragic, even murderous.

Giles is a pre-Chaplin "little man," one of our earliest abused clown heroes. At the bottom of the social hierarchy, exploited by all, he endures—and often has the last word. For the romantic critic he became the embodiment of an alienated class. Theophile Gautier called Giles: "The ancient slave, the modern proletarian, the pariah, the passive and disinherited being." Jules Janin wrote: "Giles is the common people. Giles, alternatingly joyous, sad, sick, healthy, giving beatings, receiving beatings, musician, poet, fool, always poor, as the common people are." At the end of the nineteenth century in a "surprising surprise" Hamlet appears as the double and half-brother of the tragic Pierrot, thereby establishing an unexpected geneological relationship between Giles and the Prince of Denmark.

BEAUMARCHAIS: PARADE AS ANTI-PASTORAL

The parades present a toiling world. The *commedia* characters scramble for money and position. Concentration on the material bases of civilization—food, lodging, work—make the parades inversions of the pastoral *fête galante*. Instead of the rustic games of pseudo shepherds and shepherdesses in leafy parks and bowers, the pastimes are urban swindles in the dirty streets of towns littered with undiposed human waste and peopled by sharpers, tradesmen, and the master who controls the purse strings—an acquisitive middle-class merchant. If Hermocrates in Marivaux's *The Colony* offers a portrait of the emergent bourgeois as politician, Cassander in the parades is a caricature of the prototypical bourgeois fathead who will eventually swell into Jarry's *Ubu Roi*. Whereas in Diderot's serious genre, the businessman and father of the family is the new hero treated reverentially as a progressive social force, in the parades, viewed from the high/low standpoint of common man and aristocrat, the prosperous bourgeois is a pompous money-grubber. Country born and bred, the white-faced natural fool Giles must contend against city sharks and their intrigues. Watteau's portrait of Giles is startling because it transports the ill-used valet back to an idyllic world of childhood in which he is free to dream.

No wonder that Giles, his head full of fantastic stories he has heard about fairies and pashas, is ready to believe in the magical powers of boots that will enable him to escape the constraints of his life. Such is Beaumarchais's highly sophisticated approach to the parade in *The Seven League Boots*; he uses a fairground theatrical form to show the effects of mass culture on the untutored imagination. Major types of popular literature of the period—Oriental tale, fairy tale, and travel literature—have colored the vision of this simple-minded servant to a foolish master. The fairy tales of Charles Perrault (Bluebeard, Cinderella, Sleeping Beauty, and The Seven League Boots) had first appeared in 1697 and gone through many later editions. The *Arabian Nights* in a translation by the Orientalist Antoine Galland in 1704 made the Oriental tale a household favorite. Accounts of travels to far-off lands familiarized even servants with exotic customs and manners. Nurtured on these fables and facts stranger than fiction, Giles is prepared to accept Harlequin's fabulous tales.

Beaumarchais plays off Giles's child-like imaginings, aroused by Harlequin and Leander in their colorful disguises, against the reality of money. The playwright does not specify the costumes; Chinese traveler's dress would be appropriate. In other parades, to gain access to Isabelle, Leander is disguised as a magician, Turkish merchant, Persian ambassador, and eunuch, and Harlequin even appears as a bear. As for the power of money, Beaumarchais shows strong curiosity about how people earn a living. Giving precise geographical and socio-economic details, the playwright indicates his characters' origins and source of income. Leander is the son of a rabbit skin dealer making his way in the world as a stud. A horseflayer from the Parisian suburb of Montfaucon, Cassander has inherited 20,000 crowns from his cousin, a nightsoil man, and is now speculating in real estate. Forecasting Figaro's social criticism, Harlequin complains about the ill-treatment of servants at the hands of their masters. An embittered Giles wonders how it is, in the capital of taste and fashion, that a candy-maker can go bankrupt while a cesspool cleaner makes a fortune, and asks why the rich get richer but the poor get nothing.

Although a witty spokesman for the plight of the socially deprived in his plays, Beaumarchais himself, like Cassander, was a self-made man and capitalist entrepreneur always dashing off on business trips—and the playwright moved up in the world faster and further than any of his characters. Restlessly ambitious, he tried innumerable ways of making money. Beaumarchais was a perfect eighteenth-century master of theatricalized life, a protean performer, a quick change artist at home in multiple roles, a brilliant improviser at get-rich-quick schemes.

Son of a watchmaker, at twenty-two Beaumarchais became master watchmaker to the King; he invented, designed, and patented new kinds of clockworks, including a miniature ring-watch for Madame de Pompadour, royal mistress, power behind the throne, and patroness of the arts. Artisan, courtier, composer, singer, instrumentalist, financier, diplomat, merchant, shipowner, army contractor, secret agent, publisher, pamphleteer, the creator of Figaro took on all employs, married a widow ten years his senior, acquired a title, rose in the world. The artist as opportunist and jack of all trades, Beaumarchais wrote maudlin "bourgeois dramas" as favored by Diderot because they were fashionable and would pay well. He taught harp (which he played exquisitely) to the daughters of Louis XV and organized court gaieties. During the War of Independence he financed arms shipments for the Americans, receiving a letter of thanks from the United States Congress signed by its president, John Jay, but never getting back his huge investment. He became involved in the Spanish colony of Louisiana, trading in tobacco and importing slaves (eighteenth-century humanitarian principles and commercial practice often parted company). Embroiled in constant litigation, he spent brief periods in jail, was imprisoned during the Terror, but managed to survive the Revolution by going into exile in London, Holland, and Hamburg. Beaumarchais's life was a constant drama of mixed genre, combining bourgeois tragedy, high comedy, and farce. No wonder that plays have been written about his life, including Friedrich Wolf's *Beaumarchais* (1945) depicting the author of Figaro as a vacillating liberal watching the mob on the way to the Bastille from a safe distance but unable to commit himself.

Beaumarchais's parades were written for Charles Lenormand d'Étioles, Madame de Pompadour's husband, and performed, some time between 1757 and 1763, for birthday and saint's day festivities in the chateau at Étioles near Paris. Beaumarchais acquired his taste for the parade at the age of thirteen, when, thrown out of the house by his father for debts and petty thefts, he sought refuge in the fairgrounds and considered becoming a mountebank. In the production of his parades Beaumarchais appeared as total man of the theatre. He composed the music (songs in the parades were often written to existing melodies), served as director, and along with his harp-playing sister Marie-Jeanne, acted and sang the principal roles.

Never published or subsequently mentioned by the author, the manuscripts of Beuamarchais's parades were discovered only in the 1860s and, because of their obscenity, not printed in unexpurgated form until the mid-twentieth century. In his two masterpieces—*The Barber of Seville* and *The Marriage of Figaro*—Beaumarchais subverts the proprieties of respectable comedy by introducing the boisterous sexuality of the parades. *Commedia* roles and situations are carried over in *The Barber of Seville* where Cassander appears as Bartholo and Isabelle as Rosine. Attacked by its enemies as a fairground parade not fit for the Comédie Française, *The Marriage of Figaro* uses the rollicking rhythms and aggressive comic style that Beaumarchais first developed in *The Seven League Boots*. Long before Ionesco, Beaumarchais placed in the mouths of Giles, Cassander, Leander, and Isabelle comic-strip balloons of banalities, nonsensical clichés, and garbled proverbs. In writing and staging his parades Beaumarchais discovered his true gift for farcical comedy in which satire, lazzi, song, and madcap scenic movement are blended.

COUNT JAN POTOCKI: PARADE AND HISTORICAL CHANGE

The third of our paradists, Jan Potocki (1761-1815), was a Polish nobleman who became a Tsarist agent for Russian expansionism, an extraordinary eighteenth-century traveler with seven league boots, a pioneering archeologist and geographer, and the author of a terrifying gothic novel, *The Manuscript Found in Saragossa*. Potocki lived in a period of violent social change—the American and French Revolutions and the Napoleonic Wars—and his delicate and airy parades, written during the time of the Terror, register tremors from the fall of an age-old monarchy.

A cosmopolitan aristocrat who wrote only in French, Potocki was educated in Switzerland, spoke eight languages fluently, and studied in Vienna at the Academy of Military Engineering. His interests were encyclopedic—politics, diplomacy, folklore, linguistics, zoology—and his existence nomadic. At eighteen on his travels in the Mediterranean the young Count gave chase to the Barbary pirates and was made a knight of Malta. In his early twenties he visited Tunisia, Morocco, Egypt, and Greece. Deeply committed to proper costuming and spectacle, Potocki while in Turkey adopted Turkish dress and a Turkish valet, Ibrahim Osman, from whom he was inseparable—his Giles. In 1788 the Count made a dangerous ascent over Warsaw in a balloon with Jean-Pierre-François Blanchard (an early balloonist much in vogue), accompanied by his valet Osman and his poodle Lulu.

Elected to the Polish Diet, Potocki warned of the threat posed by Prussia, set up his own publishing house, and printed revolutionary pamphlets. Dedicated to the struggle for Poland's independence, he wrote a manual on guerilla warfare and designed a special uniform for Polish partisans, which he sometimes wore. In 1789 the Count published his *Essay on Universal History* and his travel book on his journeys to Turkey and Egypt, mixing the real and the fantastic, the erudite and the swashbuckling. An excellent draftsman, the author did many sketches for his books, showing natives in indigenous costume.

In late November 1791, Potocki, a friend of Condorcet and La Fayette, appeared at the Jacobin Club in Paris, greeting the people as "the citizen count" and hailing their liberation by the revolution. But he was more impressed with the rhetoric of revolution than its substance. The theatre was his chief interest. He became a friend of the famous tragic actor François-Joseph Talma, then at the beginning of his career, and designed a Genghis Khan costume for him (Talma was then playing in Voltaire's *Orphan of China*).

Wherever he traveled, Potocki visited popular fairground theatres; in Turkey and the Near East he had been drawn to the Ottoman *Karagöz* (shadow play), in Spain to the *Entremés* of Calderón and Tirso de Molina, but it was the ribald Gallic parade that most appealed to the Francophile Polish author. In August 1792, when the Count and his wife were visiting his mother-in-law, the Princess Lubomirska, in Łańcut (a provincial town in Southeastern Poland), the right moment came for the thirty-one-year-old traveler to sit down and write his own parades. An atmosphere of joyous festivity prevailed in the Princess's magnificent palace, which contained its own private theatre (still preserved today); balls, concerts, *fête galantes* created a receptive context for the appearance on stage of the familiar *commedia* characters. Even the servants at Łańcut spoke French and many political émigrés from France (fleeing the Terror) were present as guests and took part in the performance, as did

Potocki himself and his beautiful sister-in-law, the Princess Sapieha, who played the role of Zersabelle. The following year the Count had his six parades printed in Warsaw in a limited edition.

Potocki's parades are brilliant distillations of a century-old tradition reduced to its pure theatricality. In total command of past literature of the parade, the Polish author is able to reproduce its linguistic tics and faithfully recreate many of its favorite jokes, but he has also given the old genre a modern historical consciousness. Instead of physical disguises, Potocki's *commedia* characters adopt figurative masks that serve to define their social pretensions: Giles aspires to love and marriage with Zersabelle, Leander claims to be an aristocrat, Cassander poses as a man of letters and patron of the arts or a liberal on the side of the Revolution.

In Potocki's parades, author, audience, and characters openly acknowledge a world of theatrical invention. The rules of the game, known to all participants in the festivity, are to be toyed with, commented upon, and sometimes broken. Armed with prior knowledge of the roles that they have to play, Potocki's stock characters display ironic self-awareness of the dramatic tradition to which they belong. They are self-reflexive, seasoned players who know all the moves expected of them and try out variations and new combinations. The only lesson of the parade is that, on the *commedia* stage, roles can be played and replayed, changed and interchanged. By revealing that these roles are modified according to cirumstance, the Polish paradist makes theatrical transformations aspects of historical change: social classes and relationships are in a state of flux.

After 1789, with the disappearance of the *ancien régime* and the breakdown of established order, class alignments and barriers shift rapidly. In the post-revolutionary world, the conventional parade roles have grown flexible and responsive to social change. Zersabelle now woos and weds the lowly Giles. In *Giles in Love* the white-faced clown's love for Isabelle is requited, upsetting the established rules of the traditional game. Previous Gileses had sometimes hoped to marry Cassander's daughter, but here for the first time in any parade the servant actually succeeds in winning Isabelle. In this Marivauxesque miniature surprise of love, Zersabelle watches and attempts to manipulate Giles's nascent feelings, but the shy daydreaming valet hides his passion and forces the lady to declare her love.

Cassander Supports the Revolution is an ironic commentary on the new egalitarianism. The bourgeois opportunist mouths political slogans and seeks to ally himself through marriage with the plebeian Giles (as happens in Mayakovsky's satirical comedy *The Bedbug*) to demonstrate his revolutionary zeal and make a profit. Faced with social changes brought about by the Revolution, the down-at-the-heels corporal Leander makes claims to aristocratic privileges that no longer exist and that even in the past he never enjoyed. Here Potocki parodies the revolutionary rhetoric used at the sessions of the Constituent Assembly and refers directly to the Decree of June 19,

1790, that abolished decorations, coats of arms, and titles of nobility; his double-edged irony mocks both the bourgeois-turned-citizen who hopes to profit from the Revolution and the would-be aristocrat who pretends to be a victim of it.

In Potocki's small company of *commedia* characters, the once gross and buffoonish Giles appears the equal of his better. He can see through the self-serving pretenses of the impoverished Leander and outwit his master Cassander. Giles's seeming naiveté becomes a kind of wisdom, and his absurd reasoning proves a superior kind of logic. Potocki gave the already obsolescent genre of the eighteenth-century parade a modern sensibility, making it reflect a world of shifting roles at the end of an old theatrical tradition and an old social order. In the modern Polish theatre where the mixture of political allusion, fantasy, and irony is much prized, Potocki's parades have enjoyed a number of successful productions on stage and television. The first of these, at the Dramatic Theatre in 1958, was subsequently shown in Paris, 1959, as part of the Festival of Nations, and French National Television presented Potocki's parades in 1961.

After the final partition of Poland in 1795, Count Potocki made an adjustment to historical circumstance; he became a Russian subject and abandoned his earlier struggles for Polish independence, now viewing patriotism as a sickness. Poland could be part of a vast Slavic empire under Tsarist rule. As theoretician for Russia's Oriental expansionism, Potocki agrued for military conquest, annexation, and colonization of Armenia, Georgia, Central Asia, and Afghanistan; India should be wrested from British control. Whatever countries he visited, he considered as prospective Russian colonies. Holding the eighteenth-century belief in the superiority of civilization and its rights of dominion over primitive peoples, the Polish count defended imperialist expansion as the natural prerogative of a great nation and urged Tsar Alexander I to follow the example of the Americans who forcibly took the land away from their savages. Potocki's plans for conquest in Asia became the blueprint for future Russian colonization.

In 1805 Potocki went as scientific advisor on a Russian diplomatic mission to China; the expedition, consisting of 240 members, including an orchestra, got as far as Ulan Bator in Mongolia, but never reached its destination of Peking. It failed because the Russian prince in charge was ignorant of Chinese customs and, disregarding Potocki's advice, refused to make the number of bows required by the Chinese hosts. Potocki, who knew that statecraft differs little from stagecraft, saw this incident on the Sino-Russian border as a deplorable failure of diplomacy.

In *Expedition to China* (1805) the count speculates on the origins of the Slavs and dreams of a panslavic synthesis of cultures. As the father of modern ethnography, he gives descriptions, accompanied by drawings, of modes of transport, roads, houses, clothes, weapons, educational customs, women's chores, funeral rites. Seeking out the primitive roots of present civilizations, the Polish author compares the languages, manners, and institutions of the peoples he is studying with the accounts he finds in writers of antiquity, such as Herodotus, anticipating the techniques of linguistic and cultural structuralism.

Potocki began work on his gothic novel, *The Manuscript Found in Saragossa*, in 1803 and finished it in 1815, the year in which he killed himself—out of despondency at the inactivity of his last years. This masterpiece of the fantastic was admired by Pushkin, who wrote an unfinished poem based upon it, and widely plagiarized in France; one of Washington Irving's popular ghost stories, "The Knight of Malta," is a secondhand version of an episode in Potocki's novel. In 1965 the Polish director Wojciech Has made a film of *The Manuscript Found in Saragossa*, starring Zbigniew Cybulski with music by Krzysztof Penderecki.

SURVIVALS OF THE PARADE

The parade continued on into the nineteenth century. At the outdoor performances on platform stages along the Boulevard du Temple during the early years of the Restoration, two celebrated clowns, known as Bobèche and Galimafré, popularized a new style of parade, still typified by verbal nonsense, lazzi, and vulgar jokes, but from which all the old *commedia* characters except Cassander have disapperaed. The Baron Antoine-Marie Roederer in the 1820s created parades for private performances at his own home to celebrate holidays and festive occasions and acted by members of his family. The prolific mid-nineteenth-century playwright Philippe Dumanoir cast a nostalgic look back one hundred years when he composed his *The Parades of Our Forefathers*, a pastiche of some twenty of Gueullette's farces, which was staged in Paris at the Théâtre Montansier in 1848. Giles-Pierrot and the *commedia* characters lived on in the lithographs of Daumier, the poems entitled *Fêtes galantes* of Paul Verlaine, and the saltimbanque paintings of the young Picasso. The mountebank's parade survived until the age of Georges Seurat, as can be seen in his Parisian scenes *Parade* and *Parade de Cirque* (1887-1888), and also in the parades staged at the Cercle Funambulesque in 1888 as part of the mime reveil. As late as 1917 Jean Cocteau in his collaboration with Erik Satie, Picasso, and Massine entitled *Parade* recreated a street fair theatre in Paris. The performers attempt to attract spectators inside where the real show is taking place by means of buffoonery and gags: the magic realm of Giles, Cassander, Leander, and Isabelle.

As I complete this introduction, Beaumarchais's *The Seven League Boots* is being performed at an outdoor festival in Paris.

Daniel Gerould
Summer, 1983

THE DISPUTE

A Comedy in One Act

Marivaux

CHARACTERS:

Hermiane
The Prince
Mesrou
Carise
Egle
Azor
Adine
Mesrin
Dina
Meslis
The Prince's Retinue

The action takes place in the country. Enter the Prince, Hermiane, Carise, and Mesrou.

HERMIANE: Where are we going, my lord? This strikes me as the wildest and most isolated spot in the world, and there is no sign whatsoever of the entertainment that you promised me.

PRINCE: (*Laughing.*) Everything is ready for it.

HERMIANE: I don't understand a single thing. What is this mansion where you have brought me, and which forms such a singular edifice? What is the meaning of the immense height of these different walls that surround it? Where are you leading me?

PRINCE: To see a very curious performance. You remember the question we were debating last night. In opposition to my entire court you maintained that it was not your sex, but ours that first set the example of inconstancy and infidelity in love.

HERMIANE: Yes, my lord, I still maintain it. The first inconstancy, or first infidelity, could have been begun only by someone bold enough to blush at nothing. Oh, how could you believe that of women? They have always had a natural sense of modesty and reserve which will last as long as the world itself and its inevitable decline. How could you imagine that such creatures would be the first to fall into vicious habits in affairs of the heart which demand as much audacity, as much amorous double-dealing, as much shamelessness as those we are speaking of? It is beyond belief.

PRINCE: Now, Hermiane! I find it no more likely than you do; I'm not the one you should attack on this issue; as you know, I share your opinion in opposition to all the others.

HERMIANE: Yes, you share it out of gallantry, I've noticed that.

PRINCE: If it's out of gallantry, I am not aware of it. It's true I love you, and my inordinate desire to please you could very well persuade me that you are right; but it must be affecting me in such a subtle fashion that I don't even realize it. I have no high opinion of the masculine heart, and I relinquish it to you; I consider it beyond comparison more prone to inconstancy and infidelity than the female heart; I exclude from this judgment only my own heart, and even it I would not so honor if I loved any one but you.

HERMIANE: I detect considerable irony in what you're saying.

PRINCE: If that is so, I shall soon be punished for it; because I am about to give you the wherewithal to confound me if I do not hold your view.

HERMIANE: What do you mean?

PRINCE: Yes, nature itself will be the subject of our inquiry; nature alone can resolve the question conclusively, and surely the answer will be in your favor.

HERMIANE: Explain what you mean, I do not understand you in the least.

PRINCE: To discover whether the first inconstancy or first infidelity originated with a man, as you claim—and so do I—we should have had to have been present at the beginning of the world and the infancy of human society.

HERMIANE: We should have had to, but we weren't there.

PRINCE: We are going to be there; yes, the men and women of those times, the world and its first loves are about to reappear before our very eyes exactly as they were then, or at least as they ought to have been; the adventures may not be precisely the same, but the same characters will be present; you are about to see the same emotional state, hearts every bit as naive as the first that ever were, even more naive if that is possible. (*To Carise and Mesrou.*) Carise, and you, Mesrou, leave, and when it is time for us to withdraw, give the signal we have agreed upon. (*To the retinue.*) And the rest of you, leave us now. (*Exit all but Hermiane and the Prince.*)

HERMIANE: I must admit, you have aroused my curiosity.

PRINCE: Here in brief is the situation: eighteen or nineteen years ago our current dispute arose at my father's court, grew extremely heated and lasted a long, long time. My father, of a philosophical cast of mind, but no partisan of your opinion, decided to find out what the case actually was, by means of an experiment that would be absolutely infallible. Four infants still in their cradles, two of your sex and two of ours, were brought into the forest where he had this mansion specially built for them, where each of them was separately housed, and where even at the present each resides in an area from which he or she has never strayed, with the result that they have never seen one another. So far they know only Mesrou and his sister who have brought them up, and who have always taken care of them, and who were chosen because of the color of their skin, so that their pupils would be astonished when they saw other human beings. Now for the first time we are going to allow them the freedom to leave their confines and to become acquainted with one another; they have been taught the language that we speak; we can regard the relations that they are about to establish among themselves as the first age of the world; the first loves ever are about to begin all over again, we shall see what the results will be. (*At this point the sound of trumpets can be heard.*) But let us hasten to withdraw, I hear the signal warning us, our young people are about to appear; here is a gallery that runs the entire length of the building, and from which we shall be able to see and hear them, from whatever side they leave their quarters. Let us go.

(*The Prince and Hermiane leave. Enter Carise and Egle.*)

CARISE: Come, Egle, follow me; here are new lands that you have never seen before and that you can explore without running any risk.

EGLE: I can scarcely believe my eyes! New worlds in such profusion!

CARISE: It is the same everywhere, but you do not yet know its full extent.

EGLE: So much countryside! So many dwellings! I have the feeling I'm nothing any more in such a vast open space; that both pleases and frightens me. (*She looks around and stops by a stream.*) What's this water I see flowing along the ground? I have never seen anything like that in the world I come from.

CARISE: You're right, and that's what we call a stream.

EGLE: (*Looking into the stream.*) Oh! Carise, come here, and look; there is something living in the stream that looks like a person, and she seems just as astonished to see me as I am to see her.

CARISE: (*Laughing.*) Oh, no, you're looking at yourself; streams always create that effect.

EGLE: What! That's me, that's my face?

CARISE: Of course it is.

EGLE: But do you realize it's very beautiful and offers a charming object of contemplation? What a shame I didn't know about it sooner!

CARISE: It's true that you are beautiful.

EGLE: What do you mean, "beautiful"? Simply dazzling! This discovery enchants me. (*She looks at herself again.*) The stream captures all my expressions, and I find them all appealing. You and Mesrou must have had a great deal of pleasure looking at me. I could spend my whole life contemplating myself; how I am going to love myself from this moment on!

CARISE: You are free to stroll about as you wish; I'm leaving you to go back to your quarters; I have something to do.

EGLE: Go, go, I shan't grow bored with the stream.

(*Exit Carise. Egle remains alone for an instant, then Azor appears opposite her. Egle continuing and feeling her face.*)

EGLE: I don't get tired of myself. (*And then noticing Azor, frightened.*) What's that, another person like me? . . . Don't come any closer. (*Azor stretches out his arms in admiration, smiling.*) The person is laughing, I think he's admiring me. (*Azor takes a step forward.*) Wait . . . Still his glances are quite gentle . . . Do you know how to talk?

AZOR: The pleasure of seeing you at first took away my powers of speech.

EGLE: (*Gaily.*) The person understands me, answers me, and oh, so agreeably!

AZOR: You delight me.

EGLE: So much the better.

AZOR: You enchant me.

EGLE: You appeal to me too.

AZOR: Then why do you forbid me to come any nearer?

EGLE: I don't do it with any conviction.

AZOR: Then I'm going to come closer.

EGLE: I'd like you to. (*He comes nearer.*) Stop a bit . . . How excited I am!

AZOR: I obey, because I am yours.

EGLE: The person obeys; then come here all the way, so as to be mine from closer up. (*He comes close.*) Oh! Here the person is, it's you; how well made he is! Really, you're as beautiful as I am.

AZOR: I'm overcome with joy to be near you, I give myself entirely to you, I don't know what I feel, I couldn't express it.

EGLE: Oh! It's exactly the same way with me.

AZOR: I'm happy, I'm all aflutter.

EGLE: I keep sighing.

AZOR: Being near you doesn't satisfy me, I still don't see enough of you.

EGLE: That's just what I think; but we can't see any more of each other, because we're already seeing each other.

AZOR: My heart craves your hands.

EGLE: Here, take them, my heart gives you my hands; are you any happier now? (*He holds her hands and kisses them now and then.*)

AZOR: Yes, happier, but not any calmer.

EGLE: That's what's happening to me, we're alike in every way.

AZOR: Oh, but what a difference there is! All that I am is not worth your eyes; they're so tender!

EGLE: Yours are so fiery!

AZOR: You are so dainty and delicate!

EGLE: Yes, but I assure you it suits you very well not to be as dainty and delicate as I am; I wouldn't want you to be other than you are, it's another sort of perfection; I don't deny my own; keep yours for me.

AZOR: I won't change anything, I'll always be the way I am.

EGLE: Now then, tell me, where were you before I knew you?

AZOR: In a world of my own, to which I shall never return, since you are not a part of it and I wish to hold your hands always; neither I nor my lips could get along without them any more.

EGLE: Nor could my hands get along without your lips; but I hear someone coming, those are the people from my world; so as not to alarm them, hide behind those trees; I'll call you back later.

AZOR: Yes, but I shall lose sight of you.

EGLE: No; all you have to do is look in this flowing water; my face is there, you'll see it.

(*Exit Azor, and enter Mesrou and Carise.*)

EGLE: (*Sighing.*) Oh! I'm already bored in his absence.

CARISE: Egle, something seems to have made you uneasy; what's the matter?

MESROU: Her eyes are softer than usual.

EGLE: It's because I have important news; you think there are just the three of us here, I can tell you there are four of us; I've acquired an object that held my hand just a moment ago.

CARISE: That held your hand, Egle? Why didn't you call for help?

EGLE: To save me from what? From the pleasure he was giving me? I was glad he was holding it; he had my permission to do so; he kissed it as often as he could, and no sooner did I pull my hand back than he kissed it again, as much for my pleasure as for his own.

MESROU: I know who it is, I think I even caught sight of him as he was withdrawing; that object is called a man, Azor is his name; we know him.

EGLE: Azor? What a pretty name! Dear Azor! The dear man! He'll be coming soon.

CARISE: I'm not at all surprised that he loves you and that you love him. You were made for each other.

EGLE: That's absolutely true, we figured it out all by ourselves. (*She calls him.*) Azor, my Azor, come quickly, dear man! (*Enter Azor.*)

AZOR: Oh! It's Carise and Mesrou, my friends.

EGLE: (*Gaily.*) They told me so; you were made expressly for me, and I was made expressly for you, they've been teaching me that; that's why we love each other so much: I am your Egle, you are my Azor.

MESROU: One of you is man, and the other is woman.

AZOR: My Egle, my charm, my delight and my woman!

EGLE: Here, take my hand; be consoled for having had to hide. (*To Mesrou and Carise.*) Look, that's what he did a moment ago; should I have called out for help?

CARISE: My children, I already told you, you are destined by nature to be charmed by each other.

EGLE: (*Holding his hand.*) Nothing could be clearer.

CARISE: But there is one thing that you must do if you wish to love each other forever and ever.

EGLE: Yes, I understand, we must always be together.

CARISE: Quite the contrary; from time to time you must renounce the pleasure of seeing each other.

EGLE: (*Astounded.*) What do you mean?

AZOR: (*Astounded.*) What are you saying?

CARISE: Yes, I tell you; without such separations your pleasure in seeing each other would decrease and become indifferent to you.

EGLE: (*Laughing.*) Indifferent, indifferent, my Azor! Ha! ha! ha! . . . What a funny idea!

AZOR: (*Laughing.*) How little she understands such things.

MESROU: Don't laugh, she's giving you very good advice, only by practicing what she's been telling you and by separating for certain periods have Carise and I been able to go on loving each other.

EGLE: In your case, I can well believe it; that's probably good for people like you who are both so black, you must have run away in a terrible fright when you first saw each other.

AZOR: The best you could hope for was to endure each other's presence.

EGLE: And you'd soon be repelled by the sight of each other if you never separated, because you have nothing beautiful to offer another person; I, for example, love both of you, but when I don't see you, I can get along quite well without you: I feel no need of your company; and why don't I? Because you don't charm me; while on the other hand, Azor and I charm each other; he is so beautiful, I am so dazzling and attractive that we become carried away just looking at each other.

AZOR: (*Taking Egle's hand.*) Egle's hand, you see, her mere hand, when I don't hold it, I suffer; and when I do hold it, I'm in agony if I don't kiss it; and when I've kissed it, I'm still in agony.

EGLE: The man is right; I feel everything he's been telling you; that's the point we've reached; and you talk about our pleasure without knowing the first thing about it; we don't understand it, but we feel it; it is boundless.

MESROU: We don't suggest that you separate for more than two or three hours a day.

EGLE: Not for a single minute.

MESROU: So much the worse for you.

EGLE: You're beginning to irritate me, Mesrou; will we become ugly just because we see each other? Will we stop being charming?

CARISE: No, but you will stop feeling that you are.

AZOR: Come now! What will prevent us from feeling we're charming since we actually are charming?

AZOR: Egle will always be Egle.

EGLE: Azor will always be Azor.

MESROU: I agree, but who can tell what may happen? Suppose for example that I become as attractive as Azor and that Carise becomes as beautiful as

Egle?

EGLE: What would that have to do with us?

CARISE: Perhaps then, tired of seeing each other, you might both be tempted to abandon the other and fall in love with us.

EGLE: Why would we be tempted? Does any one give up what he loves? That's not logical, is it? Azor and I love each other, there's nothing more to be said; become as beautiful as you like, what does it matter to us? That's your business; ours is already settled.

AZOR: They'll never understand the first thing about it; you have to be us in order to know what it's actually like.

MESROU: If that's what you say.

AZOR: My love is my entire life.

EGLE: Do you hear what he's saying, his entire life? How could he possibly give me up? He needs me to live, and I need him.

AZOR: Yes, my entire life; how is it possible for someone to be so beautiful, to have such beautiful eyes, such beautiful lips, and such beautiful everything?

EGLE: I so like to have him admire me!

MESROU: It's true that he adores you.

AZOR: Oh! That's the right way to put it, I adore her! Mesrou understands me, I adore you.

EGLE: (Sighing.) Adore me then, but give me a chance to breathe; oh!

CARISE: What tenderness! I'm enchanted by it myself! But the only way to preserve it is by believing us; and if you have the good sense to make such a resolve, here, Egle, give this to Azor; it's something to help him endure your absence.

EGLE: (Taking portrait that Carise gives her.) What's this? I recognize myself; it's me again, and much better than in the waters of the stream; all my beauty is there; it's me; what pleasure to come across oneself everywhere! Look, Azor, look at my charms.

AZOR: Oh! It's Egle, it's my dear woman; there she is, except the real one is even more beautiful. (He kisses the portrait.)

MESROU: At least it offers a likeness of her.

AZOR: Yes, it makes one want the real Egle.

EGLE: I find only one fault with it; when he kisses it, my copy gets everything.

AZOR: (Taking her hand, which he kisses.) Let's do away with that fault.

EGLE: Now then, I want something like that to keep me entertained.

MESROU: Choose either his portrait or your own.

EGLE: I'm keeping both of them.

MESROU: No, you must decide between the two, if you please; I'm planning to keep one of them.

EGLE: Well, in that case I don't need you in order to have Azor, because I already have his portrait in my mind; so give me my own portrait, and then

I'll have both of them.

CARISE: Here it is in a different form. This is called a mirror; you just press this spot to open it. Goodbye, we'll be back to get you in a while; but, for goodness sake, give some thought to short separations. (*Exit Carise and Mesrou.*)

EGLE: (*Trying to open the box.*) You see; I can't open it; you try, Azor; here's where she said to press.

AZOR: (*Opens it and looks at himself.*) Well, look at that! It's only me, I guess; it's my face that the near-by stream first showed me.

EGLE: Oh! Oh! What do I see now! No! It's not you at all, dear man, it's more me than ever; it really is your Egle, the real one; come here and look.

AZOR: Oh! Yes, it's you; wait, now it's both of us, it's partly you and partly me; I'd prefer it to be only you, because I get in the way and prevent myself from seeing all of you.

EGLE: Oh! I'm perfectly glad to see a little of you too; you don't spoil anything; come over here close again, keep in your place.

AZOR: Our faces are about to touch, now they're touching; what happiness for mine! What delight!

EGLE: I can feel that you're close, and I like it.

AZOR: What if our lips were to touch. (*He steals a kiss from her.*)

EGLE: (*Turning toward him.*) Oh! You're disturbing us; now I see only myself; what a charming invention a mirror is!

AZOR: (*Taking the mirror from Egle.*) Oh! The portrait is not such a bad thing either. (*He kisses it.*)

EGLE: Carise and Mesrou are good people, after all.

AZOR: They only want what's good for us; I was going to speak to you about them and the advice they gave us.

EGLE: You mean, about those separations? I've been thinking it over too.

AZOR: Yes, my Egle, what they predict frightens me a bit; I don't have any apprehensions on my account; but don't you go and get tired of me, I'd be driven to despair.

EGLE: Watch out for yourself, don't you weary of adoring me; honestly, beautiful as I am, your fears alarm me.

AZOR: All right! You don't have any cause to worry . . . What's on your mind now?

EGLE: Look here, after thinking it all over, I've made my decision: let's endure the pain; let's part for two hours; I prefer your heart and your admiration to your presence, even though that is very dear to me.

AZOR: What! To leave each other!

EGLE: Oh! If you don't agree right this minute, in another moment I won't want to either.

AZOR: Heavens! I don't have the courage.

EGLE: That makes things worse, I tell you mine is waning.

AZOR: (*Weeping.*) Goodbye, Egle, since we have to.

EGLE: You're weeping? Well, then in that case, stay since there isn't any more danger.

AZOR: But what if there were!

EGLE: Then go away.

AZOR: I'm on my way. (*Exit Azor.*)

EGLE: (*Alone.*) Oh, he's gone, I'm alone, I don't hear his voice any more, all I have is the mirror. (*She looks at herself in it.*) It was wrong of me to send my man away; Carise and Mesrou don't know what they are talking about. (*Looking at herself.*) If I had contemplated myself a little more carefully, Azor wouldn't have had to go. He had no need of any separation to love forever what I see there . . . All right, I'll go sit by the stream; that will give me one mirror more.

(*Enter Adine.*)

EGLE: But what's this I see? Another person!

ADINE: Oh! Oh! What's that new object over there? (*She comes forward.*)

EGLE: She's been looking me over carefully, but she's not filled with wonder; she's no Azor. (*She looks at herself in the mirror.*) Still less is she an Egle . . . Yet I do believe she's comparing herself with me.

ADINE: I don't know what to think of that creature, I don't know what she's lacking; there's something insipid about her.

EGLE: She's not a type that appeals to me.

ADINE: Has she a tongue? . . . Let's see . . . Are you a person?

EGLE: I certainly am, I'm very much a person.

ADINE: Well, in that case, don't you have anything to tell me?

EGLE: No, usually people don't give me a chance to, people say things to me first.

ADINE: But don't you find me charming?

EGLE: Find you charming? I'm the one others find charming.

ADINF: What! You're not perfectly delighted to see me?

EGLE: Sorry! I'm neither perfectly delighted nor annoyed; it's a matter of indifference to me.

ADINE: Now that's unheard of! You have me in full view, I'm showing myself, and you don't feel anything! You must be looking somewhere else; contemplate me a little more attentively; there now, what do you think of my looks?

EGLE: But why all this talk about you? Who's concerned with you? I tell you people notice me first, people always tell me what they think of me; that's how it happens, and you expect me to spend my time gazing at you while I'm here to be looked at!

ADINE: Of course I do; the greatest beauty waits for others to notice her and be thunderstruck.

EGLE: Well, then, go ahead and be thunderstruck.

ADINE: Don't you understand what I'm saying? You've just been told that the greatest beauty waits for others to pay attention to her.

EGLE: You've been answered that she's waiting.

ADINE: But if it isn't me, where is she? Yet I am the source of admiration for three other people who live in the world.

EGLE: I don't know your people, but I do know that there are three other people whom I delight and who treat me as a wonder.

ADINE: And I for my part know I am so beautiful, so beautiful that I charm myself every time I look at myself; you see how it is.

EGLE: What sort of a story is that you're telling me? But you can take it from me that I never contemplate myself without being thoroughly enchanted.

ADINE: Thoroughly enchanted! It's true that you're passable, and even rather pretty; I do you justice, I'm not like you.

EGLE: (*Aside.*) I could beat her with the greatest pleasure for that justice of hers.

ADINE: But to think that you could enter into competition with me is ridiculous; you have only to take a look at the two of us.

EGLE: But it was precisely when I took a look that I discovered how ugly you are.

ADINE: You think so, do you! It's because you're envious of me and won't allow yourself to admit I'm beautiful.

EGLE: Only your face won't allow me to admit it.

ADINE: My face! Oh! I'm not worried about my face, because I've seen it; go ask the waters of the flowing stream what my face is like; ask Mesrin—he adores me.

EGLE: The waters of the stream, which mock you, will show me that nothing is as beautiful as I am, and they have already done so; I don't know exactly what a Mesrin is, but he would stop looking at you if he once saw me; I have an Azor who is worth far more than he, an Azor whom I love, who is almost as admirable as I am, and who says that I am his entire life; *you* aren't anyone's entire life; and then I have a mirror that offers me conclusive proof of everything my Azor and the stream have been saying; could anything be more decisive than that?

ADINE: (*Laughing.*) A mirror! You have a mirror too! Well now! What good does it do you? Let you look at yourself? Ha! ha! ha!

EGLE: Ha! ha! ha! Didn't I foresee that I wouldn't like her?

ADINE: (*Laughing.*) Look, here's a better mirror; come and learn to know yourself and to keep your mouth shut.

(*Carise appears in the distance.*)

EGLE: (*Ironically.*) Cast your eyes on this mirror; you'll discover your own mediocrity, and the modesty it is fitting for you to show in my company.

ADINE: Go your way; once you deny yourself the pleasure of contemplating me, you're of no interest to me, I'm not speaking to you any more.

(*They no longer look at each other.*)

EGLE: I for my part am ignoring that you're here.

(*They move apart.*)

ADINE: (*Aside.*) She's crazy!

EGLE: (*Aside.*) She's imagining things! From what world does something like that come?

CARISE: Why are you two standing there so far apart without even exchanging a single word?

ADINE: (*Laughing.*) There's a new creature here, whom I've just met, and my beauty is driving her to despair.

EGLE: What would you say about a wishy-washy object like that, a ridiculous sort of person like that who tries to strike me with wonder, who asks me what I feel when I see her, who wants me to take pleasure in looking at her, who tells me: "Hey! Contemplate me now! Hey! What do you think of my looks?" and who claims to be as beautiful as I am!

ADINE: I never said that, I said more beautiful, as one glance in the mirror will show.

EGLE: (*Showing her mirror.*) Just let her look at herself in this mirror if she dares!

ADINE: I ask nothing more of her than a single glance in my mirror, which is the truthful mirror.

CARISE: Calm down, don't get so excited; you should be grateful for the opportunity to get acquainted. Why don't we all live together harmonious-ly? You can be companions, and add the pleasure of seeing one another to the sweetness of both being adored, Egle by the handsome Azor whom she holds dear, Adine by the handsome Mesrin whom she loves; come on, make up.

EGLE: Then let her get over her exaggerated notions of her own beauty which irritate me.

ADINE: Look, I know the way to make her listen to reason; all I need to do is take her Azor away from her, not that I care anything about him, except to make her keep quiet.

EGLE: (*Incensed.*) Where is that half-witted Mesrin of hers? She'll regret it if I meet him! So long, I'm going; I simply can't stand her.

ADINE: Ha! ha! ha! . . . My praiseworthy qualities arouse her antipathy.

EGLE: (*Turning around.*) Ha! ha! ha! What a frightful scowl! (*Exit Egle.*)

CARISE: Let her say whatever she wants.

ADINE: Of course, you're right; I only feel sorry for her.

CARISE: We must be going now; it's time for your music lesson; I won't be able to give it to you if you're late.

ADINE: I'm right behind you, but I just caught sight of Mesrin; I have to have a word with him.

CARISE: You just left him.

ADINE: I'll be only a minute, not a second more. (*Calls.*) Mesrin!

MESRIN: (*Running up.*) What! It's you, my Adine has come back! What joy you bring me! I could hardly wait!

ADINE: Oh, no, put off your joy a bit; I haven't come back yet, I'm about to leave again; I'm here quite by chance.

MESRIN: Then it must have been by chance that you're here with me.

ADINE: Listen, just listen to what happened to me.

CARISE: Make it brief, I have something else to do.

ADINE: I'm almost done. (*To Mesrin.*) I ask you, am I beautiful?

MESRIN: Beautiful! Are you beautiful?

ADINE: He has no hesitations; he reports what he sees.

MESRIN: Are you divine, are you beauty itself?

ADINE: Oh, yes, I never had any doubts about it; and yet it seems that you, Carise, and I are all mistaken; I'm actually ugly.

MESRIN: My Adine!

ADINE: Yes, your Adine; after leaving you, I discovered a new person who comes from another world; instead of being thunderstruck by me, instead of being entranced as you are and as she ought to have been, this new person wanted *me* to be charmed by *her*, and, when I refused, she accused me of being ugly . . .

MESRIN: You're putting me into a rage!

ADINE: She even claimed that you'd leave me once you had seen her.

CARISE: She said that because she was offended.

MESRIN: But . . . is she really a person?

ADINE: She says she is, and she even looks like one, more or less.

CARISE: She's a person too.

ADINE: She's sure to come back, and I absolutely insist that you treat her with contempt; when you meet her, I hope that you'll be appalled.

MESRIN: She must be frightful.

ADINE: Her name is . . . wait, her name is . . .

CARISE: Egle.

ADINE: That's right, she's an Egle. Now here's what she looks like: she has a cross, sullen face, not as black as Carise's, but not as white as mine either; I'd be hard pressed to say what color it is.

MESRIN: But it's not appealing?

ADINE: Oh, not in the least! It's a nondescript color; she has eyes, how can I describe them to you? Eyes that fail to give pleasure, that stare, and nothing more; a mouth neither large nor small, a mouth that serves for speaking; a figure straight and flat, and yet which would be almost like ours, if she were well built; she has hands that move restlessly about, fingers that are long and thin, I think; and a voice that's shrill and harsh; oh, you'll recognize her all right!

MESRIN: I can almost see her now; let me take care of her: she'll need to be sent off to some other world after she's been thoroughly shamed by me.

ADINE: Thoroughly humiliated, thoroughly abused.

MESRIN: And thoroughly ridiculed; oh, don't be upset, and give me that hand.

ADINE: Oh, take it! My hand is yours and yours alone. (*Mesrin kisses her hand.*)

CARISE: (*Taking away Adine's hand from Mesrin.*) Come on, there's nothing more to be said; we must be going.

ADINE: When he's finished kissing my hand.

CARISE: That'll do now, Mesrin; I'm in a hurry.

ADINE: Farewell to all I hold most dear, I won't be long; don't forget to avenge me.

MESRIN: Farewell to all that charms me! I am furious.

(*Exit Adine and Carise. Enter Azor. Mesrin's first words are spoken alone, as he goes over the portrait of Egle painted by Adine.*)

MESRIN: Color neither black nor white, figure straight and flat, mouth only for speaking . . . Where am I going to find her? (*Seeing Azor.*) But I see someone; it's a person like me; could it be Egle? No, it can't be, it's not deformed.

AZOR: (*Looking him over.*) You're like me, that's how it seems to me?

MESRIN: That's what I was thinking too.

AZOR: You're a man, aren't you?

MESRIN: I've been told I am.

AZOR: I've been told that too.

MESRIN: Who told you? Do you know people?

AZOR: Oh yes, I know all of them, two blacks and a white girl.

MESRIN: It's the same with me; where do you come from?

AZOR: I come from the world.

MESRIN: From my world?

AZOR: Oh, I don't know about that, there are so many worlds!

MESRIN: Does it matter? The way you look suits me fine; put your hand in mine; we should love each other.

AZOR: Sure we should, you make me feel good; I enjoy seeing you even if you don't have any charms.

MESRIN: You don't either; I don't care for you, except that you're great fun.

AZOR: That's just how it is; I consider you the same way, you're a good pal, that's what I am too; I don't pay any attention to your face.

MESRIN: Yes! That's true! It's your good humor that makes me like you. Say, by the way, do you take your meals?

AZOR: Every day.

MESRIN: What do you know! So do I; let's take them together, as a way of having fun together, so as to keep our spirits high; all right, that's for a little later; we'll laugh, we'll jump, won't we? I'm jumping already. (*He jumps.*)

AZOR: (*He jumps too.*) I am too, and there'll be the two of us, perhaps four, because I'll tell my white girl about it, has she got a face, you should see it! Ha! ha! She's got a face that's worth the two of us together.

MESRIN: Oh, I can well believe it, pal; because you're nothing at all, nor am I either, compared to another face I know that we'll put here along with us; she thrills me, her hands are so sweet and white, and she lets me kiss them to my heart's content!

AZOR: Hands, pal? Talk about hands! Doesn't my white girl have hands that are perfectly heavenly, and don't I get to caress them as much as I want? I'm awaiting the return of those hands.

MESRIN: Good for you; I just left my hands, and I have to leave you too on account of a small piece of business. Stay here until I come back with my Adine, and let's jump for joy one more time to celebrate this happy encounter. (*They both jump, laughing all the while.*) Ha! ha! ha!

(*Enter Egle.*)

EGLE: (*Coming over to them.*) What's going on here that's so enjoyable?

MESRIN: (*Seeing her.*) Oh, look at that beautiful object that's been listening to us!

AZOR: That's my white girl, that's Egle.

MESRIN: Egle, is that the cross face?

AZOR: I'm so happy!

EGLE: (*Drawing closer.*) Is this a new friend who's suddenly appeared to us out of nowhere?

AZOR: Yes, we've just become pals, his name is man, and he comes from a near-by world.

MESRIN: My, but it's easy to enjoy oneself in this world!

EGLE: Are you enjoying yourself more than in your world?

MESRIN: I certainly am!

EGLE: Well, in that case, man, the only thing to do is to stay here.

AZOR: That's what we're saying, because he's a thoroughly good sort and always joyous; I love him, not the same way I love my ravishing Egle whom I adore, whereas I don't even pay much attention to him, it's just that I seek out his company to talk about you, about your lips, about your eyes, about your hands, for which I have been longing. (*He kisses one of her hands.*)

MESRIN: (*Taking her other hand.*) Then I'm going to take the other hand. (*He kisses this hand, Egle laughs, and says nothing.*)

AZOR: (*Regaining possession of that hand from Mesrin.*) Now watch it, this isn't your white girl, it's mine; these two hands are my property, you don't have any rights to them.

EGLE: Oh, he's not doing any harm; but anyhow, Azor, run along; you know perfectly well that a separation was necessary; and ours hasn't lasted long enough yet.

AZOR: What! I haven't seen you for I don't know how many hours.

EGLE: You're wrong; it hasn't lasted long enough, I tell you; I'm quite capable of keeping count; once I've decided on something, I like to stick to it.

AZOR: But you'll be left all by yourself.

EGLE: That's just fine! I'll be glad to be.

MESRIN: Don't torment her, pal.

AZOR: I think you're angry with me.

EGLE: Why do you insist on opposing me? Didn't they tell you that there is nothing as dangerous as seeing each other?

AZOR: Perhaps that's not true.

EGLE: But I suspect it's no lie.

(*Carise appears in the background and listens.*)

AZOR: I'm leaving to please you, but I'll be back soon; come on, pal, since you had something you had to do, come along with me and help me pass the time.

MESRIN: Yes, but . . .

EGLE: (*Smiling.*) What?

MESRIN: I've been walking around for quite a while.

EGLE: He should rest.

MESRIN: And I would have kept the beautiful woman from growing bored.

EGLE: Yes, he'd be able to.

AZOR: Didn't she say she wanted to be alone? If that weren't so, I'd prevent her from being bored better than you ever could. Let's be going!

EGLE: (*Aside, with malice.*) Let's be going!

(*Azor and Mesrin leave.*)

CARISE: (*Draws near and looks at Egle who is lost in thought.*) What are you mulling over?

EGLE: I'm trying to figure out why I'm not in a good mood.

CARISE: Did you run into some serious trouble?

EGLE: It's not so much serious trouble as it is a case of mental confusion.

CARISE: What's the cause?

EGLE: You were telling us a little while ago that in matters of the heart you can never tell what will happen?

CARISE: That's true.

EGLE: Well, there you have it! I don't know what's happening to me.

CARISE: But what's the matter with you?

EGLE: I think I'm upset with myself, or upset with Azor; I don't know who to be cross with.

CARISE: Why be upset with yourself?

EGLE: Because I meant to love Azor forever and ever, and I'm afraid I may not make it.

CARISE: Could that be possible?

EGLE: Yes, and I blame Azor for it, because his behavior and attitude are the cause of all the trouble.

CARISE: I suspect you're trying to pick a quarrel with him.

EGLE: All you have to do is keep answering me that way, and I'll soon be upset with you too.

CARISE: You really are in a bad humor; but what has Azor done to you?

EGLE: What has he done to me? We agree to separate; he leaves, he comes back right away, he'd like to stay here with me all the time; in the end, what you predicted would happen to him will happen to him.

CARISE: What do you mean? That you'll stop loving him?

EGLE: I'm afraid so; if our pleasure in seeing each other doesn't last when indulged in too frequently, is that *my* fault?

CARISE: You told us that could never happen.

EGLE: Stop needling me; what did I know then? I said that out of ignorance.

CARISE: Egle, it can't be his over-eagerness to see you that has made you change your opinion of Azor; you haven't known him long enough for that.

EGLE: It's not been such a short time either; we've already had three conversations together, and evidently the length of the meetings has a negative effect.

CARISE: There again, you're not telling what his real offense is.

EGLE: Oh, he's committed at least one and maybe even two, he's guilty of I don't know how many offenses: first of all, he crossed me, because my hands are mine to dispose of, I think, they belong to me, and yet he forbids anyone else to kiss them!

CARISE: And just who wanted to kiss them?

EGLE: A pal Azor discovered quite recently, he's called man.

CARISE: And he's attractive?

EGLE: Oh! Charming, nicer than Azor, and what's more he offered to stay and keep me company, and that demented Azor wouldn't allow him to enjoy either my hand or my company, quarreled with him, and took him away abruptly without consulting my wishes. How dare he! So I'm not the mistress here? Doesn't he have any confidence in me? Is he afraid someone else will love me?

CARISE: No; but he feared that his friend appealed to you.

EGLE: Well, in that case he has only to appeal to me more, because when it comes to being loved, I welcome the opportunity, I declare it openly, and if instead of one pal, he had a hundred pals, I'd like them all to love me; that's my pleasure; he wants to keep my beauty all for himself, whereas I maintain that it's for the entire world.

CARISE: Hold on, your dislike for Azor doesn't follow from the things you've just been saying, but from the fact that now you like his friend better than you like him.

EGLE: Do you think so? You could well be right.

CARISE: Now tell me, aren't you a little ashamed of being so fickle?

EGLE: I suppose I am; the mess I'm in makes me feel embarrassed; it's another case of ignorance.

CARISE: It's no such thing; you promised so often to love Azor faithfully!

EGLE: Wait a minute, when I promised to, he was the only one there was; he should have stayed the only one; I hadn't counted on the pal.

CARISE: Admit those are trumped-up reasons; you refuted them in advance a few minutes ago.

EGLE: It's true I don't take them too seriously; still there is one excellent reason, the pal is more than a match for Azor.

CARISE: You're wrong again on that point; it's not that he's more than a match for Azor, it's simply that he has the advantage of being a newcomer.

EGLE: But that's a considerable advantage; doesn't it count for anything to be a newcomer? Doesn't it count for anything to be someone else? At least that's pretty nice; those are virtues lacking in Azor.

CARISE: You can add that this newcomer will fall in love with you.

EGLE: That's just it, he'll fall in love with me, I certainly hope so; that's yet another good quality he has.

CARISE: Whereas Azor is not capable of falling in love with you.

EGLE: That's right; because he already loves me.

CARISE: What strange reasons for being fickle! I should be willing to bet that you are not happy about it.

EGLE: I'm not happy about anything; on the one hand, changing the object of my affection causes me pain, on the other hand, it gives me pleasure; I cannot prevent the one any more than the other; they are both of real consequence; to which of the two am I most obligated? Should I cause myself pain? Should I give myself pleasure? I defy you to say which.

CARISE: Consult your own kind heart; you will feel that it condemns your inconstancy.

EGLE: Didn't you hear what I've been saying? My kind heart condemns it, my kind heart approves of it; the only thing to do is to choose the easiest solution.

CARISE: You know the decision you should make? To flee from Azor's pal. Now come along; you'll spare yourself a painful struggle.

EGLE: (*Seeing Mesrin coming.*) Yes, but we're fleeing a bit too late; here comes the struggle, the pal is on his way.

CARISE: Never mind, make an effort, be brave! Don't look at him.

(*Enter Mesrou and Mesrin.*)

MESROU: (*From a distance, trying to hold back Mesrin, who gets free.*) He's getting away from me, he wants to be unfaithful; keep him from coming any nearer.

CARISE: (*To Mesrin.*) Don't come any closer.

MESRIN: Why not?

CARISE: Because I forbid you to; Mesrou and I should have some authority over you; we're your masters.

MESRIN: (*In revolt.*) My masters? What's a master?

CARISE: Well, all right, I don't order you now, I beg you, and the beautiful Egle joins her prayer to mine.

EGLE: Me! Never, I won't join in any such prayer.

CARISE: (*To Egle, aside.*) Let's withdraw; you're still not yet sure that he loves you.

EGLE: Oh, I've little hope that he doesn't; we have only to ask him what his feelings are. What do you want most, pretty pal?

MESRIN: To see you, to contemplate you, to admire you, to call you "my soul."

EGLE: You see, he talks about his soul; do you love me?

MESRIN: With all my heart.

EGLE: Didn't I tell you?

MESRIN: Do you love me too?

EGLE: I'd be glad to get out of having to if I could, because of Azor, who's counting on me.

MESROU: Mesrin, follow Egle's example; don't be unfaithful.

EGLE: Mesrin! The man's name is Mesrin!

MESRIN: Oh, yes, that's right.

EGLE: Adine's friend?

MESRIN: I was her friend, but I don't need her portrait any more now.

EGLE: (*Takes the portrait.*) Her portrait and Adine's friend! That's something else to his credit; listen, Carise, he has too many good qualities, there's no way of resisting him; Mesrin, come here so that I can love you.

MESRIN: Oh, how sweet the hand that I possess!

EGLE: Oh, how matchless the friend that I gain!

MESROU: Why abandon Adine? Do you have any cause to complain of her?

MESRIN: No, it's this beautiful face that bids me leave her.

EGLE: He has eyes, it's that simple.

MESRIN: Oh, I don't deny I'm unfaithful, but I'm helpless to do anything about it.

EGLE: Yes, I incite him to it; we spur each other on.

CARISE: She and Azor will be in despair.

MESRIN: It can't be helped.

EGLE: What's the remedy?

CARISE: If you like, I know the way to end their sorrow along with their tender feelings.

MESRIN: Well then, do it!

EGLE: Oh, no, I'm looking forward to having Azor regret he's lost me; my beauty deserves no less; there's no harm in having Adine sigh a bit either, to teach her a lesson for knowing herself so little.

(*Enter Azor.*)

MESROU: Here is Azor.

MESRIN: The pal makes me feel uneasy, he'll be absolutely dumbfounded.

CARISE: From the look on his face, you might think he forsees the wrong you're doing him.

EGLE: Yes, he's sad; and doesn't he have good reason to be! (*Azor comes forward shamefaced; she continues.*) Are you quite upset, Azor?

AZOR: Yes, Egle.

EGLE: Very much?

AZOR: I couldn't be more so.

EGLE: That's easy to see; tell me, how did you find out that I love Mesrin?

AZOR: (*Astounded.*) What?

MESRIN: Yes, pal.

AZOR: Egle loves you! So she doesn't care for me any more?

EGLE: That's true.

AZOR: (*Relieved.*) Well, so much the better; go on and love him, I don't care for you any more either; wait for me, I'll be right back.

EGLE: Stop, what do you mean? You don't love me any more? What's this all about?

AZOR: (*Going out.*) You'll find out soon enough. (*Exit Azor.*)

MESRIN: You're trying to call him back, I think; tell me why? What do you need to talk to him for now that you love me?

EGLE: Just let me do what I want; if I can see him again, it will only make me love you more; it's only that I don't want to lose anything.

CARISE AND MESROU: (*Laughing.*) Ho! Ho! Ho! Ho!

EGLE: This is no laughing matter!

(*Enter Azor with Adine.*)

ADINE: (*Laughing.*) Hello, Egle the beautiful! When you feel like looking at yourself, come speak to me about it; I have your portrait, someone turned it over to me.

EGLE: (*Throwing Adine her portrait.*) There, I give you back yours, it's not worth my while to keep it.

ADINE: What! My portrait, Mesrin! How did she get it?

MESRIN: I gave it to her.

EGLE: All right, Azor, come here so I can speak to you.

MESRIN: So you can speak to him! Where does that leave me?

ADINE: Move over this way, Mesrin; what are you doing there? You've been saying the strangest things, in my opinion.

(*Enter the Prince, Hermiane, Meslis, and Dina.*)

HERMIANE: (*Entering post-haste.*) No, let me go now, Prince; I do not wish to see any more; as far as I'm concerned, Adine and Egle are insufferable; in those two fate has seen fit to show us what will always be the most detestable among my sex.

EGLE: Who are all those creatures coming here and scolding us? I'm going to get out of here. (*Egle and the others try to get away.*)

CARISE: Stay, all of you, don't be afraid; here are some new pals; don't frighten them, and let's see how they react.

MESLIS: (*Stopping in the middle of the stage.*) Oh, dear Dina, what a lot of people!

DINA: Yes, but they are no concern of ours.

MESLIS: How true, not one of them is anything like you. Oh, it's you, Carise and Mesrou; are all the others men or women?

CARISE: They are half and half; these are the women, and those are the men; look, Meslis, and see if among the women you don't find someone who appeals to you more than Dina; if you do, she'll be given to you.

EGLE: I'd certainly like his friendship.

MESLIS: Don't bother liking it, you won't have it.

CARISE: Choose another.

MESLIS: I thank you; I don't dislike them, but I don't care for them, there is only one Dina in the world.

DINA: (*Putting her arm on his.*) How nicely you said that!

CARISE: Now you, Dina, study the men.

DINA: (*Taking Meslis by the arm.*) What more is there to see? Let's be on our way.

HERMIANE: The adorable child! I shall look after her fortune.

PRINCE: And I shall do the same for Meslis.

DINA: We have all we need in each other.

PRINCE: You will not be separated; Carise, see to it that they are kept apart from the rest, and have the others placed according to my orders. (*To Hermiane.*) Neither sex has any cause to reproach the other: the virtues and vices are equally divided between them.

HERMIANE: Oh, I beg you, don't put them both on the same plane: your sex displays a horrible faithfulness; men are fickle for no reason at all, without even seeking a pretext.

PRINCE: I admit it, the conduct of your sex is at least more hypocritical, and for that reason more decent; women make more of a fuss about their consciences than men do.

HERMIANE: Believe me, we have no reason to treat these matters lightly. Let us go.

END

THE DISPUTE (directed by Patrice Chéreau)

THE DISPUTE (directed by Henryk Tomaszewski)

Claude Bricage

Marek Grotowski

THE COLONY

A Comedy in One Act and in Prose

Marivaux

CHARACTERS:

Arthenice, noblewoman
Madam Sorbin, wife of a commoner engaged in one of the handicrafts
Mr. Sorbin, husband of Madam Sorbin
Timagenes, nobleman
Lina, Madam Sorbin's daughter
Persinet, young man and commoner, Lina's sweetheart
Hermocrates, at first taken for a nobleman, but actually a bourgeois philosopher
A Band of Women, equally divided between nobles and commoners

The action takes place on an island where all the characters have found a haven.

ARTHENICE: Now then! Madam Sorbin, or rather my companion, because that is what you are, since the women of your class have just invested you with the same power that the noblewomen have conferred on me, let us join hands, unite forces, and together show but one mind.

MADAM SORBIN: (*Giving her her hand.*) The result: here there is but one woman and one idea.

ARTHENICE: We are now faced with the greatest task that our sex has ever undertaken, and this comes at the critical moment in the world most favorable to discussing our rights vis-a-vis the men.

MADAM SORBIN: Oh, this time, Gentlemen, we shall have an equal voice.

ARTHENICE: Since we were forced to take refuge with them on this island where we have settled, the government of our homeland has ceased to exist.

MADAM SORBIN: Yes, there must be a totally new government here on the island, and the hour has come; we are now in a position to obtain justice and to rise up out of the degrading subservience that has been imposed on us ever since the world began; better die than endure our wrongs any longer.

ARTHENICE: Very well, do you really feel that you have the fortitude answering to the grandeur of your calling?

MADAM SORBIN: Listen, at present I care not a straw for my life; I commit myself totally to the cause. Madam Sorbin wishes to live in the annals of history and not in this base world.

ARTHENICE: I guarantee that your name will be immortalized.

MADAM SORBIN: Twenty thousand years from now, we shall still be the news of the day.

ARTHENICE: And even if we do not succeed, our granddaughters will.

MADAM SORBIN: I tell you the men will never be the same again. Besides, although you're the one offering me advice to stand firm, there's a certain Mr. Timagenes here who's been chasing after you; is he still giving chase? He hasn't won your heart, has he? That would be a glaring instance of human weakness, take care.

ARTHENICE: Who is Timagenes, Madam Sorbin? I know him no longer, not since our plan has been conceived; be steadfast and think only of imitating me.

MADAM SORBIN: Who? Me! And where's the problem? I only have a husband, what does it cost to leave something like that? It's no love affair.

ARTHENICE: Oh, there I quite agree with you!

MADAM SORBIN: Now then! You know that in a moment the men are going to assemble in the tents in order to choose from their midst two men who will make laws for all of us; the drum has been beaten to convene the assembly.

ARTHENICE: Well, what of it?

MADAM SORBIN: Well, what of it? We have only to have the drum beaten too in order to instruct our women to disregard the rules and regulations of these gentlemen, and immediately to draw up in due form an act of separation from the men, who as yet suspect nothing.

ARTHENICE: That was my very thought, except that instead of a drum, I wanted to have our decree proclaimed to the sound of the trumpet.

MADAM SORBIN: Yes, to be sure, the trumpet is a fine thing and most appropriate.

ARTHENICE: Look, there's Timagenes and your husband passing by without seeing us.

MADAM SORBIN: Evidently they're on their way to the Council Meeting. Is it your wish that we call them?

ARTHENICE: Why not? We shall question them about what is happening. (*She calls Timagenes.*)

MADAM SORBIN: (*Calls out also.*) Stop there, man of ours!

(*Enter Timagenes and Mr. Sorbin.*)

TIMAGENES: Oh, forgive me, beautiful Arthenice, I did not think that you were so near-by.

MR. SORBIN: What is it you want, wife of mine? We are in a hurry.

MADAM SORBIN: Oh, now, now, hold your horses, I simply want to see you, Mr. Sorbin, and say how do you do. Have you nothing to communicate to me, by chance or not by chance?

MR. SORBIN: No, what do you want me to communicate to you, unless it's about the state of the weather or the time of the day?

ARTHENICE: And you, Timagenes, what news can you tell me? Is there talk about the women amongst you men?

TIMAGENES: No, Madam, I know nothing concerning the women; not a word has been said on that subject.

ARTHENICE: Not a word, that's a fine way to treat the matter.

MADAM SORBIN: Wait a bit, the proclamation will wake you up.

MR. SORBIN: What do you mean by that proclamation of yours?

MADAM SORBIN: Oh, nothing! I was just talking to myself.

ARTHENICE: Well, now, Timagenes, tell me: where are you two going with such serious looks on your faces?

TIMAGENES: To the Council Meeting where we have been called, and where the nobility and all the bourgeois notables on the one hand and the common people on the other threaten to appoint us—this honest man and me—to work on drafting the laws, and I confess that my unfitness for the assignment already makes me tremble.

MADAM SORBIN: What, my husband, are you going to be a law-giver?

MR. SORBIN: Unfortunately, that's what's being bruited about, and what causes me such great uneasiness.

MADAM SORBIN: Why, Mr. Sorbin? Although you are dense and by nature a bit slow-witted, I've always acknowledged you've got a lot of plain good sense that will come in very handy in that business; and then I'm convinced that those gentlemen will have the good judgment to ask some of the women to help them, as is only reasonable.

MR. SORBIN: Oh, stop that blabber about your women, this is a fine time to joke!

MADAM SORBIN: But really, I'm not joking.

MR. SORBIN: Then have you gone crazy?

MADAM SORBIN: Good gracious, Mr. Sorbin, you are an elected representative of the common people totally lacking in good manners; but luckily, that will come to an end with a decree; you see, I'm drawing up laws too.

MR. SORBIN: (*Laughing.*) You! Ho! Ho! Ho! Ho!

TIMAGENES: (*Laughing.*) Ho! Ho! Ho! Ho! . . .

ARTHENICE: What's so funny about that? She's right, that's what she'll do, and so will I.

TIMAGENES: You, Madam?

MR. SORBIN: (*Laughing.*) Laws!

ARTHENICE: Most certainly.

MR. SORBIN: (*Laughing.*) Well, all right, good for you, do whatever you want, have your fun, play the fool; but for the time being spare us your little nonsense, it's too ridiculous for a serious moment like this.

TIMAGENES: Why? Merriment is always in season.

ARTHENICE: Merriment, Timagenes?

MADAM SORBIN: Our little nonsense, Mr. Sorbin? Take care, we'll teach you a little nonsense.

MR. SORBIN: Let's leave these female wags, my lord Timagenes, and be on our way. Goodbye, wife, many thanks for your help.

ARTHENICE: Wait, I may have a thought or two to communicate to the right honorable Elected Representative of the nobility.

TIMAGENES: Speak, Madam.

ARTHENICE: A modicum of attention; the mighty and the humble, nobles, bourgeoisie, and common people, we have all been forced to leave our homeland to escape death or to flee slavery at the hands of the enemy who conquered us.

MR. SORBIN: I have the impression we're being harangued. Could we put it off until a little later? We don't have any time to spare now.

MADAM SORBIN: Quiet, lout.

TIMAGENES: Let's hear what they have to say.

ARTHENICE: Our ships brought us to this savage country, and the country has proved to be good.

MR. SORBIN: Only thing wrong here is that our wives babble too much.

MADAM SORBIN: (*Growing angry.*) Can't you keep still!

ARTHENICE: The plan to stay here took shape, and as we all came here in total disarray, and as fortune made us all equal, as no one has the right to command, and as everything is in a state of confusion, so now we must have rulers, we must have one chief or even several of them, we must have laws.

TIMAGENES: Now, that is just what we are going to provide for, Madam.

MR. SORBIN: There's going to be all that in short order, they're waiting for us to put it into effect.

ARTHENICE: Who is us? Who do you mean by us?

MR. SORBIN: Well, good gracious, we mean us, there's not anyone else it can be.

ARTHENICE: Not so fast, just who is going to make those laws, with whom will they originate?

MR. SORBIN: (*Contemptuously.*) With us.

MADAM SORBIN: With the men!

MR. SORBIN: Obviously.

ARTHENICE: And from among whom will these rulers, or this ruler, be selected?

MADAM SORBIN: (*Contemptuously.*) From among the men.

MR. SORBIN: Oh, obviously.

ARTHENICE: Who will the ruler be?

MADAM SORBIN: A man.

MR. SORBIN: Well, who else could it be?

ARTHENICE: And always it's men and never women. What's your view on the subject, Timagenes? Because the plain sense of your deputy assistant falls short of comprehending what I am trying to say.

TIMAGENES: I must confess, Madam, that I don't understand what the difficulty is either.

ARTHENICE: You don't understand? That will do, leave us.

MR. SORBIN: (*To his wife.*) Tell us what it's all about.

MADAM SORBIN: You can ask me that? Go away.

TIMAGENES: But, Madam . . .

ARTHENICE: But, Sir, you are irritating me.

MR. SORBIN: (*To his wife.*) What does she mean?

MADAM SORBIN: Just go take your man's face somewhere else.

MR. SORBIN: Who are they so upset with?

MADAM SORBIN: Always men and never women, and they don't understand us.

MR. SORBIN: Well, what of that?

MADAM SORBIN: (*Slapping her husband's face.*) Take that! The oaf, that's what of it.

TIMAGENES: You distress me, Madam, if you allow me to leave without informing me what sets you against me.

ARTHENICE: Leave, Sir, you'll find out when you come back from your Council Meeting.

MADAM SORBIN: The drum will tell you the rest, or else the announcement at the sound of the trumpet.

MR. SORBIN: Fife, trumpet, or bugle, I don't care in the least; let's go, Mr. Timagenes.

TIMAGENES: In my present state of anxiety, Madam, I shall return as soon as I possibly can.

(*Exit Timagenes and Mr. Sorbin.*)

ARTHENICE: Not to understand us is a new way of abusing us.

MADAM SORBIN: It's their time-honored habit of being arrogant, handed down from father to son, that blocks their mental powers.

(*Enter Persinet and Lina.*)

PERSINET: (*To Madam Sorbin.*) I come to you, revered and future mother-in-law; you have promised me the charming Lina; and I am most impatient to be her husband; I love her so passionately that I shall not be able to endure such love without marriage.

ARTHENICE: (*To Madam Sorbin.*) Get rid of that young man, Madam Sorbin; present circumstances compel us to break off all relations with his entire species.

MADAM SORBIN: You are right, such an acquaintanceship is no longer suitable.

PERSINET: I await your answer.

MADAM SORBIN: What are you doing here, Persinet?

PERSINET: Dear me, I'm here to plead with you, and I am escorting my peerless Lina.

MADAM SORBIN: Go back.

LINA: He's to go back! Oh, how come, mother?

MADAM SORBIN: I want him to go away, he has to, the situation requires it, it's a matter involving affairs of state.

LINA: Couldn't he follow us from a distance?

PERSINET: Yes, I'd be glad to stay meekly in the rear.

MADAM SORBIN: No, there'll be no staying at all, I won't allow it; be off with you, don't come near us until there's peace.

LINA: Farewell, Persinet, till we meet again; let's not provoke my mother any further.

PERSINET: But who shattered the peace? Cursed war, while I wait for it to finish, I shall go off by myself to grieve to my heart's content. (*Exit Persinet.*)

LINA: Why do you mistreat him, mother? Don't you want him to love me any more or to marry me?

MADAM SORBIN: No, daughter, we are in a situation where love is nothing but sheer idiocy.

LINA: Oh, dear me, what a pity!

ARTHENICE: And marriage, such as it has been until now, is nothing more than pure enslavement which we are abolishing, my fair young child; (*to Madam Sorbin*) to console her, we have to educate her a bit as to the facts.

LINA: Abolish marriage! And what will be in its place?

MADAM SORBIN: Nothing.

LINA: That's giving it short shrift.

ARTHENICE: You know, Lina, until now women have always been submissive to their husbands.

LINA: Yes, Madam, but that custom has never prevented anyone from falling in love.

MADAM SORBIN: I forbid you to have anything to do with love.

LINA: When one is in love, how is it possible to get out? I did not choose love, love chose me, and I cannot help submitting.

MADAM SORBIN: What! Be submissive! Good heavens, do you have the petty soul of a servant? Submissive! Can such a word come from a woman's mouth? So that I won't ever hear you utter that horror again, know that we are staging a rebellion.

ARTHENICE: Don't lose your temper, she didn't take part in our deliberations, on account of her age, but I can vouch for her once she knows how matters stand. I assure you that she'll be delighted to have as much authority as her husband in her little domestic world, and when he says, "I want it this way," she'll be thrilled to be able to reply, 'Well, I don't want it that way."

LINA: (*Weeping.*) I won't ever need to do that; Persinet and I always want the same thing; we've agreed to between ourselves.

MADAM SORBIN: Watch out with that Persinet of yours; if you don't have any higher goals, I'll expel you from the noble corps of women; stay with my comrade and me and learn to esteem your own importance; and above all, let there be no more tears which bring shame to your mother and lower our worth as women.

ARTHENICE: I see some of our friends coming; they seem to have something to tell us, let's find out what they want of us.

(*Enter four women, two of whom each hold a bracelet of striped ribbon.*)

ONE OF THE DEPUTIES: Revered companions, the sex that has appointed you its leaders, and chosen you to defend it, has just deemed it proper, in a new deliberation, to confer upon you tokens of your eminence, and we bring you these on behalf of the entire assembly. We are charged, at the same time, to swear to you in the name of all the women total obedience, once you have placed your hands in ours and sworn an inviolable loyalty to our sex: two essential articles that were at first overlooked.

ARTHENICE: Illustrious deputies, we would willingly have dispensed with the pomp in which you clothe us. It would have been enough for us to be adorned in our virtues; it is by these that we should be known.

MADAM SORBIN: Never mind, let's take them anyhow; that'll make two ornaments rather than one.

ARTHENICE: We accept, however, the distinction with which you honor us, and we shall execute the vows, whose omission has been most judiciously noted; I begin.

(*She places her hand in the hand of one of the deputies.*)

I solemnly swear to live to uphold the rights of my oppressed sex; I consecrate my life to the glory of women; I swear it on my self-respect as a woman, on my unyielding pride of heart, which is a gift from heaven, about that there can be no mistake; finally I swear it on my rebellious state of mind which always guided me in my marriage, and saved me from the disgrace of obeying my late boor of a husband; I have finished. You are next, Madam Sorbin.

MADAM SORBIN: Draw near, my daughter, and become forever celebrated, solely for having been present at such a memorable event as this.

(*She places her hand in the hand of one of the deputies.*)

Here are my words: you will be on a par with the men, they will be your comrades, and not your masters. Everywhere Madam will equal Sir, or I shall die in the attempt. I swear it by the most resounding oath that I know: by this head of iron that will never bend, and that until now no one can boast of having ever subjugated, you have only to ask to learn if that is so.

ONE OF THE DEPUTIES: Now listen to what all the women whom we represent swear to you in their turn. We shall see the world end, the race of men die out before we cease to obey your commands; here now is one of our companions who loses no time in coming here to acknowledge your pre-eminence.

WOMAN: (*Entering.*) I hasten to come pay hommage to our sovereigns, and to place myself under their laws.

ARTHENICE: Let us kiss and embrace, my friends; our mutual oath has just imposed on us weighty duties, and to incite you to fulfill yours, I think it fitting at this time to paint you a vivid picture of the abasement in which we have languished until this very day; in so doing we shall only be following the practice of all political leaders.

MADAM SORBIN: It's called exhorting the troops before the battle.

ARTHENICE: But common decency requires that we be seated, we can speak more at ease in that position.

MADAM SORBIN: There are benches over there, we have only to bring them closer. (*To Lina.*) All right, little girl of mine, look lively.

LINA: I see Persinet passing by, he's stronger than I am, and he'll help me, if you like.

ONE OF THE WOMEN: What! Will we employ a man?

ARTHENICE: Why not? I'd say that it augurs well for our enterprise to have a man serve us.

MADAM SORBIN: That's the right way to put it; in the present situation, it will bring us good luck. (*To Lina.*) Call that domestic over here.

LINA: (*Calling.*) Persinet! Persinet!

PERSINET: (*Running up to Lina.*) What is it, my love?

LINA: Help me push these benches over here.

PERSINET: With pleasure, but don't you touch them, your little hands are too delicate, let me do it.

(*He moves the benches up; Arthenice and Madam Sorbin, after a few civilities, sit down first; Persinet and Lina sit down together at the very end of one of the benches.*)

ARTHENICE: (*To Persinet.*) I'm amazed at the liberty you're taking, little boy. Get out of there, you're not needed any more.

MADAM SORBIN: You've performed your service, Be on your way.

LINA: He hardly takes up any room at all, he uses only half the space I do.

MADAM SORBIN: Out you go, we're telling you.

PERSINET: That's really very harsh. (*Exit Persinet.*)

ARTHENICE: (*After having coughed, cleared her throat, and spit.*) The oppression in which we live under the sway of our tyrants, for being so time-honored, has not become any more reasonable; we must not expect that the men will improve of their own accord; even though the inadequacy of their laws may punish them for having framed them to suit themselves and without our guidance—nothing will bring them round to the justice that they owe us, they have even forgotten that they deny it to us.

MADAM SORBIN: That's how the world goes, you have only to open your eyes and see.

ARTHENICE: The way things are arranged, it's been decided once and for all that we don't have any common sense, and now it's taken as so self-evident that we're not even allowed to appeal the decision.

ONE OF THE WOMEN: Why, what do you expect? From cradle on we're yelled at, "You're not fit to do anything, don't try to do anything, you're not good for anything except being quiet and behaving yourselves." That's what they told our mothers who believed it and repeated it to us; we've had these pernicious ideas dinned into our heads; we're soft, we get lazy, we're led like sheep.

MADAM SORBIN: Oh, as for me, I'm only a woman, but since I reached the age of reason, the sheep never thought that was right.

ARTHENICE: "I am only a woman," says Madam Sorbin, that's amazing!

MADAM SORBIN: It's due to that sheepishness still within us.

ARTHENICE: We must harbor a highly commendable distrust of our own intellectual capacities to have adopted barbarous language like that. Try to find any men who would say such things about themselves; that's beyond them. Still, let's face the truth: you are only a woman, you say? Well, what would you like to be that would be better?

MADAM SORBIN: Oh, I'll stick with what I am, Ladies, I'll stick with what I am. We have the best of it, and I praise heaven for having made me part of it all, I have been crowned with honors, and I express my unparalleled thanks to providence for it.

ONE OF THE WOMEN: Dear me! That's absolutely right.

ARTHENICE: We should be duly impressed with what we are worth, not out of pride, but out of gratitude.

LINA: Oh, if you heard Persinet on that subject, you'd see how impressed he is with our qualities.

ONE OF THE WOMEN: Persinet has nothing to do with this, it's unseemly to mention him.

MADAM SORBIN: Quiet, little girl, hold your tongue, and keep your ears open; excuse her, Ladies; continue, comrade.

ARTHENICE: Let us examine what we are, and stop me if I say too much; what is a woman, judging solely by what one can see? Truly, could it not be said that the gods have made her the object of their loving care?

ONE OF THE WOMEN: The more I reflect on it, the more convinced I am.

ONE OF THE WOMEN: That's indisputable.

ANOTHER WOMAN: Absolutely indisputable

ANOTHER WOMAN: It's a fact.

ARTHENICE: Simply looking at her is a pleasure to the eyes.

A WOMAN: You could say a sheer delight.

ARTHENICE: Allow me to finish.

A WOMAN: Let's stop interrupting her.

ANOTHER WOMAN: Yes, let's listen.

ANOTHER WOMAN: Let's have a little quiet.

ANOTHER WOMAN: It's our leader who's speaking.

ANOTHER WOMAN: And she speaks well.

LINA: I'm not saying a word.

MADAM SORBIN: Will you all shut up? Because I'm beginning to lose my patience!

ARTHENICE: I resume: Simply looking at her is a pleasure to the eyes; graces and beauty, in various shapes and forms, contend as to which will lavish the most charms on her face and her figure. Now, who can tell the number and variety of these charms? They can be felt, but our means of expression fal far short of doing justice to them. (*Here all the women hold their heads high.*) Woman has a noble aspect, and yet the softness of her mien is enchanting. (*Here the women adopt a soft look.*)

A WOMAN: That's us.

MADAM SORBIN: Shush!

ARTHENICE: Hers is a beauty proud, yet delicate; it instills a respect that none dares lose unless she leads the way; it inspires a love that cannot remain silent; to say that she is beautiful, that she is adorable, is only to begin to paint her portrait; to say that her beauty beguiles, that it is domineering, touching, ravishing, is to say, roughly, what anyone can see, and not even to graze the surface of what everyone thinks.

MADAM SORBIN: And what's unprecedented is that they can live with all those beautiful things as if it were nothing worth noticing; that's the most surprising, but what I'm saying isn't meant to interrupt, so not another word!

ARTHENICE: Let us now turn to the mind, and see to what extent our intelligence has seemed formidable to our tyrants; judge of this matter by the precautions they have taken to stifle our intellect and to keep us from using our minds; what is it these gentlemen condemn us to? To spinning, to the distaff, to the management of their household finances, to the frightful drudgery of domestic life, in a word, to knitting our lives away.

A WOMAN: In truth, that cries out for vengeance.

ARTHENICE: Or, we're expected to know how to pass judgment on matters of dress, to entertain them at their evening dinner parties, to inspire them with pleasurable emotions, to reign in a world of trifles, and ourselves to be no more than the foremost of all the trifles; these are all the functions they leave us here on earth; despite the fact that we are the ones who have civiliz- ed them, who have taught them manners, who have refined the ferocity of their souls; and that without us the Earth would be little more than a dwell- ing place for savages who would not merit the name of men.

ONE OF THE WOMEN: Oh, the ingrates! All right, Ladies, from this moment on let us do away with evening dinner parties.

ANOTHER: And as for passions, let them fend for themselves.

MADAM SORBIN: To make a long story short, let them do their own spinning.

ARTHENICE: It's true that they treat us as charmers, we are stars, they ascribe to us the hues of lilies and roses, we are celebrated in poetry in which the outraged sun pales with shame in our presence, and as you see, that's quite something; and then the transports, the ecstasies, the fits of despair with which we are regaled when we feel so inclined.

MADAM SORBIN: To tell the truth, those are sweets that one gives to children.

ANOTHER WOMAN: Sweets, on which we have been nourished for more than six thousand years.

ARTHENICE: What is the result? Out of pure naiveté we cling to the vile honor of pleasing them, and we quite innocently fritter away our time being co- quettes, because that is what we are, it must be admitted.

A WOMAN: Is it our fault? That's all we have to do.

ARTHENICE: That's undoubtedly so; but the amazing thing is that the superi- ority of our soul is so invincible, so tenacious, that it withstands everything that I have just been saying, it shoots forth and cuts through the degrada- tion into which we fall; we are coquettes, agreed, but even our coquet- tishness is a marvel.

A WOMAN: Oh, everything that originates in us is perfect.

ARTHENICE: When I think of all the genius, all the wisdom, all the intelligence that each one of us puts into coquetry without the slightest effort, and that we can put nowhere else but there, it is immense; there goes into coquetry more depth of thought than would be needed to govern two worlds like ours, and all that intelligence is pure waste.

MADAM SORBIN: (*In a rage.*) This world of ours profits nothing from it; that's what is so deplorable.

ARTHENICE: All that intelligence accomplishes nothing except to turn the heads of small minds who are easy prey, and winning us some idiotic com- pliments which their vices and their giddiness, not their reason, lavish on us; their reason has never offered us anything but insults.

MADAM SORBIN: All right then, no quarter; I vow I'll be ugly, and our first decree will be that we all try to be equally ugly. (*To Arthenice.*) Would you support that, comrade?

ARTHENICE: I agree to it.

ONE OF THE WOMEN: To be ugly? If you ask me, that's the wrong way to go about it.

ANOTHER WOMAN: I'll never be of that opinion either.

ANOTHER WOMAN: Well, who could be? It's unheard of! To make oneself ugly to take revenge on men? Look here, quite on the contrary, let's make ourselves more attractive, if that is possible, so that they will be even sorrier to have lost us.

ANOTHER WOMAN: Yes, so they'll sigh more than ever at our feet, and die of grief when they find themselves rejected; that's a more sensible way to express our indignation, and you're on a false track, Madam Sorbin, on a completely false track.

MADAM SORBIN: Blah, blah, blah, take my word for it, by making ourselves more attractive we only sink back again; of twenty gallants who die at our feet, sometimes there's not a single one who is not rescued from danger, usually they are all saved; those dying suitors are apt to get the best of us, I'm well acquainted with our disposition, and our decree stands; we'll make ourselves ugly; besides, that won't be such a great pity, Ladies, and you won't lose more by it than I will.

A WOMAN: Oh, hold on, that's easy for you to say, you don't have much at stake; you're already fairly far along in that direction.

ANOTHER: It's hardly astonishing that you'd dispose of your attractions so readily.

ANOTHER: You'd never be taken for a heavenly body.

LINA: By heaven, nor you for a star either.

A WOMAN: Will you listen to that little feather-brain prattling away.

MADAM SORBIN: Oh, good gracious, I really am dumbfounded; now, tell me, you conceited ninnies, do you think you're pretty?

ANOTHER: Well, I like that! But if we look like you, what's the need to make ourselves ugly? How would we go about it?

ANOTHER: It's true the Sorbin woman can talk on the subject without a worry.

MADAM SORBIN: What's that, the Sorbin woman? Call me, the Sorbin woman?

LINA: My mother, the Sorbin woman!

MADAM SORBIN: Then who here will deserve to be called madam; to lose respect for me in that fashion?

ARTHENICE: (*To the other women.*) You're wrong, my dear, and I find Madam Sorbin's proposal most wise.

A WOMAN: Oh, I can believe it; you have no more to lose than she does.

ARTHENICE: What does that mean? To attack me personally?

MADAM SORBIN: But just look at those frights, with their delusions of beauty; yes, Madam Arthenice and I who are superior to you, wish, order, and insist that you dress badly, that you wear your headdresses askew, and that you blacken your faces in the heat of the sun.

ARTHENICE: And to satisfy these women here, our edict exempts only them, they will be permitted to beautify themselves, if they can.

MADAM SORBIN: Oh, that's telling them; yes, keep all your trinkets, corsets, ribbons, along with your affected looks and grimaces which are so laughable, and your little sandals or slippers into which you squeeze a foot that simply won't fit and that you vainly try to make slender despite its size, adorn yourselves, adorn yourselves, it's a matter of no importance.

ONE OF THE WOMEN: Good heavens! How coarse she is! We made a fine choice in her!

ARTHENICE: Be off with you; your oaths bind you, obey; I adjourn the meeting.

ONE OF THE WOMEN: Obey? She's giving herself great airs.

ONE OF THE WOMEN: The only thing to do is complain, we have to protest.

ALL THE WOMEN: Yes, let's protest, let's protest, let's object.

MADAM SORBIN: I confess my fingers are itching to get hold of them.

ARTHENICE: Be off with you, I tell you, or I'll have you put under arrest.

ONE OF THE WOMEN: (*Leaving with the others.*) It's your own fault, Ladies, I didn't want that commoner's wife or that princess either, I didn't want any part of them, but you wouldn't listen to me. (*Exit all the women.*)

LINA: Dear me! Mother, to make it all up, let us keep our sandals and our corsets.

MADAM SORBIN: Keep quiet, I'll dress you in a sack if you talk back to me.

ARTHENICE: Let us take a moderate course, they're not in their right minds; we have a decree to formulate, let us go get it ready.

MADAM SORBIN: Let's go; (*to Lina*) and as for you, wait here until the men come out of their Council Meeting, and take care you don't talk to Persinet if he comes; do you promise you won't?

LINA: But . . . yes, mother.

MADAM SORBIN: And come warn us as soon as the men appear, without a minute's delay.

(*Exit Madam Sorbin and Arthenice.*)

LINA: (*Alone for a moment.*) What commotion! What disorder! When will I ever be married at this rate? I'm completely at a loss.

(*Enter Persinet.*)

PERSINET: Come now, Lina, my dear Lina, tell me what calamity has struck me down; how come Madam Sorbin has driven me away? I'm still all atremble, I can't go on, I'm dying.

LINA: Oh, my! What a dear little man, if I could only speak to him in his affliction.

PERSINET: But why can't you? I'm right here.

LINA: But I've been forbidden to, I'm not even allowed to look at him, and I'm sure I'm being spied on.

PERSINET: What! Cut me off from your eyes?

LINA: It's true he can speak to me, I haven't been ordered to stop him from doing that.

PERSINET: Lina, my Lina, why do you keep me at such a distance from you? If you don't take compassion on me, I haven't long to live; at this very moment I need a glance to keep me going.

LINA: Yet if, in this case, a look was the only thing that could save Persinet, oh, I wouldn't let him die, no matter what my mother says. (*She looks at him.*)

PERSINET: Oh, what blessed medicine! It makes me feel alive again; do that once more, my love, another roll of the eye to bring me back to full health.

LINA: And if one look is not enough, I'll give him two or three, as many as he needs. (*She looks at him.*)

PERSINET: Oh, I've recovered somewhat; now tell me the rest; but speak to me closer up and not as though I weren't here.

LINA: Persinet does not know that we have staged a rebellion.

PERSINET: A rebellion against me?

LINA: And that affairs of state are what is thwarting us.

PERSINET: Good grief! What are they getting mixed up in?

LINA: And that the women have decided to govern the world and make laws.

PERSINET: Am I preventing them?

LINA: He does not know that shortly we will be ordered to break off all contact with the men.

PERSINET: But not with the boys?

LINA: And that we will be ordered to be ugly and ill dressed in the presence of the men, lest they take pleasure in seeing us, and all that to be done by means of a proclamation at the sound of the trumpet.

PERSINET: I defy all the trumpets and all the proclamations in the world to stop you from being pretty.

LINA: The result is I shall no longer have either sandals or corset, and my headdress will be worn askew and I may well be dressed in a sack. You can imagine what I shall look like.

PERSINET: You will always look like yourself, my dear little sweetheart.

LINA: But here are the men coming out of the meeting, I'm off to warn my mother. Oh, Persinet! Persinet! (*She runs off.*)

PERSINET: Wait a minute, I understand now; oh, cursed laws, I'll take my complaint to these gentlemen.

(*Enter Mr. Sorbin, Hermocrates, Timagenes, and Another Man.*)

HERMOCRATES: No, lord Timagenes, we could not have chosen better; the common people did not hesitate to pick Mr. Sorbin, the rest of the citizens were unanimous for you, and we are in good hands.

PERSINET: Gentlemen, allow me to make an urgent plea: I appeal to you, Mr. Sorbin; these affairs of state are taking my life blood, I'm overwhelmed with grief; you think you have a son-in-law, and that's where you're mistaken; Madam Sorbin has sent me packing quite unceremoniously until there is peace; you've been sent packing too, people of our stamp are no longer wanted, anything resembling a man's face is banished; we're going to be cut off at the sound of the trumpet, and I request your protection when the insurrection breaks out.

MR. SORBIN: What do you mean, my son? What's this insurrection?

PERSINET: It's a riot, a conspiracy, a disturbance, an uprising directed against the government of the realm; you'll find out that the women have gathered in a group to be ugly; they're going to give up slippers, there's even talk of changing out of dresses, and wearing a sack, and of putting their bonnets on sideways to displease us; I saw preparations being made for a great conference, I even moved the benches up to facilitate the conversation; I tried to sit down, I was chased away like a scamp; the world is going to collapse, and all because of your laws, which those worthy ladies want to make in collaboration with you, and half the framing of which I advise you to grant them, as is only just.

TIMAGENES: Is what he's telling us possible?

PERSINET: What are laws? The merest trifle in comparison to the endearments of those ladies!

HERMOCRATES: Be off with you, young man.

PERSINET: Has everyone taken leave of his senses? Wherever I go, I'm told, "Go away"; I don't understand what's going on.

MR. SORBIN: So that's what they meant a while ago?

TIMAGENES: You see for yourself.

HERMOCRATES: Fortunately, the incident is more comic than dangerous.

ANOTHER MAN: That's certainly true.

MR. SORBIN: My wife is stubborn, and I'll wager she stirred up the whole thing; but wait for me here; I'm going to see what it's all about, and I'll put a stop to that folly once I adopt my voice of authority; I'll shut them up for you; don't go away, Gentlemen. (*He goes out to one side.*)

TIMAGENES: What surprises me is that Arthenice is a party to it.

(*Enter Arthenice, Madam Sorbin, A Woman with a drum, and Lina, holding a proclamation.*)

ARTHENICE: Gentlemen, deign to answer our question: you are about to make regulations for the republic, won't we be working jointly on it? What do you plan to have us do?

HERMOCRATES: Nothing, as usual.

ANOTHER MAN: In other words, to marry when you are young girls, obey when you are wives, and run your households; that we can't take away from you, it's your destiny.

MADAM SORBIN: Is that your last word? Beat the drum; (*and to Lina*) and you, go post the decree on that tree. (*The drum is beaten and Lina posts the decree.*)

HERMOCRATES: But what kind of bad joke is this? Speak to them, lord Timagenes, find out what's it all about?

TIMAGENES: Are you willing to explain yourselves, Madam?

MADAM SORBIN: Read the proclamation, it explains everything.

ARTHENICE: It will inform you that we wish to be involved in everything, to be partners in everything, to exercise with you all offices, including those of finance, justice, and the sword.

HERMOCRATES: The sword, Madam?

ARTHENICE: Yes, the sword, Sir; remember, until now we've only been cowards by upbringing.

MADAM SORBIN: Death and confusion! Give us arms, and we'll be more bloodthirsty than you; in a month I want us to be able to handle a pistol as skillfully as a fan: the other day I shot at a parrot, sure as I'm talking to you.

ARTHENICE: It's all only a matter of practice.

MADAM SORBIN: It's the same with being a Judge and presiding at a court of law, or being Prime Minister, State Councillor, Provincial Governor, General, or Lawyer.

A MAN: Women lawyers?

MADAM SORBIN: Look here, we don't have the gift of gab, is that the problem?

ARTHENICE: I don't think that you'll contest the fact that we're smooth talkers.

HERMOCRATES: You can't mean it, the solemnity of the bench and the decorum of the bar would never accord with a lawyer's square cap being placed on top of a woman's starched bonnet.

ARTHENICE: And just what is a lawyer's square cap, Gentlemen? What gives it greater importance than another form of headdress? Besides, it's not part of any pact made by us, any more than your legal code is; until now it is your justice and not ours; justice that seeks favor in our beautiful eyes, when we deign to look in that direction, and if we share in instituting the laws, we shall see what we'll make of that justice, as well as of the lawyer's square cap, which might well become octagonal if we're provoked; neither the widow nor the orphan will lose thereby.

A MAN: And that won't be the only thing that you'll put on our foreheads.

MADAM SORBIN: Oh, what a clever bit of wit; but to end this discussion, there won't be any softening of our demands; if you think there will, you have only to read our edict, your dismissal is at the bottom of the page.

HERMOCRATES: Lord Timagenes, issue your orders, and deliver us from all this wrangling.

TIMAGENES: Madam . . .

ARTHENICE: Sir, I have only one more word to say, take it to heart; there is no nation that does not complain of the shortcomings of its government; where do these shortcomings originate? It is because the earth has been denied our intellect in instituting its laws, it is because you make no use of that half of the human mind we possess, and because you employ only your own, which is the weaker half.

MADAM SORBIN: That's exactly it, for want of cloth, the coat goes short.

ARTHENICE: The kind of marriage that takes place between men and us should also be consummated between their thoughts and ours; that's what the gods intended, but their plans have not been fulfilled, and that's the reason for the imperfection of the laws; the universe is the victim of this lack and by resisting you we serve its cause. I have said what I have to say; there is no point in answering me, make your decision, we give you one hour more, after that the separation becomes irrevocable, if you do not yield; follow me, Madam Sorbin, let us leave.

MADAM SORBIN: (About to leave.) Our share of mental abilities bids yours farewell.

(Enter Mr. Sorbin as the women are about to leave.)

MR. SORBIN: (Stopping Madam Sorbin.) Oh, so I've found you, Madam Sorbin, I was looking for you.

ARTHENICE: Finish with him; I'll come back and get you in a moment.

MR. SORBIN: (To Madam Sorbin.) To tell the truth, I am most charmed to see you, and your behavior is highly diverting.

MADAM SORBIN: So it gives you pleasure, does it, Mr. Sorbin? So much the better, I'm still only at the preamble.

MR. SORBIN: You told this boy you meant to stop associating with people of his stamp; enlighten us a bit as to what you mean by that?

MADAM SORBIN: Certainly, I mean by that everything that looks anything like you.

MR. SORBIN: Just why are you saying that, Madam Bonnet?

MADAM SORBIN: Because it's what I think and what will be made good, Mr. Hat.

TIMAGENES: Hold on now, Madam Sorbin; is it fit and proper for a woman as sensible as you to discard every last shred of the respect she owes her husband?

MADAM SORBIN: Listen to him, with his man's lingo! It's just because I am sensible that things are happening as they are. You say that I owe my husband respect, but he owes me every bit as much; when he pays me that debt, I'll pay him, that's exactly what I came here to demand of him.

PERSINET: Well then, pay her, Mr. Sorbin, pay her, let's all pay what we owe.

MR. SORBIN: The brazen-faced hussy!

HERMOCRATES: You see clearly that this undertaking cannot succeed.·

MADAM SORBIN: Will we perhaps be lacking in courage? Oh, no, certainly not, we've taken our measures, everything is settled, our things are packed.

TIMAGENES: But where will you go?

MADAM SORBIN: Straight ahead always.

TIMAGENES: What will you live on?

MADAM SORBIN: On fruit, on grasses, on roots, on shellfish, on nothing at all; if necessary, we'll fish, we'll hunt, we'll become savages again, and our life will end with honor and glory, and not in the degrading subservience in which you men want to keep people of our caliber.

PERSINET: And who excite my admiration.

HERMOCRATES: This is perfect madness. (To Mr. Sorbin.) Answer her.

MR. SORBIN: What can I do? It's folly all right, but let's come back to our senses; do you know, Madam Sorbin, that I intend to take the bull by the horns?

MADAM SORBIN: Oh, my! The poor man with his horns, he's a fine one to talk like that; what drivel!

MR. SORBIN: Drivel! To whom are you talking, if you please? Am I not the elected representative of the people? Am I not your husband, your master, and the head of the family?

MADAM SORBIN: You are this, you are that . . . Do you think you are going to make me tremble with the catalogue of your various titles that I know better than you do? I advise you to sound the warning; look, wouldn't you say he was up in the clouds? You are the elected representative of the men, and I am the elected representative of the women; you are my husband, and I am your wife; you are the master, and I am the mistress; as for being head of the family, let's go easy there, there are two heads here, you are one, and I am the other, and so we are absolutely even.

PERSINET: What she's saying is pure gold, honestly it is.

MR. SORBIN: All the same, the respect a woman owes . . .

MADAM SORBIN: All the same, respect is pure idiocy; let's finish this discussion, Mr. Sorbin, the right honorable elected representative, husband, master, and head of family; all that is well and good; but listen to me for the last time, that's what you'd better do; let us say that the world is a farm, the gods above are its lords and masters, and you men, ever since there has been life, have always been its tenant farmers all by yourselves, and that is not just, give us our share of the farm; you govern, we'll govern; you obey, we'll obey; we'll share and share alike both profit and loss; we can be masters and servants jointly; do this, my wife; do that, my man; that's how it should be said; that's the mold in which the laws should be cast; that's what we want, we insist on it; we are determined to achieve it; don't you want that? As your wife, who loves you, and whom you should love, as your companion, your good friend and not your little servant, unless you are her little servant, I announce to you and give you notice in this case that you have no wife any longer, that she is leaving you, that she is breaking up the household and giving you back the key to the dwelling; I have spoken for myself; my daughter, whom I see over there and whom I am about to call, will speak for herself. All right, Lina, come closer, I have done my duty, you do yours, give us your opinion on the current state of affairs.

LINA: My dear mother, my opinion . . .

TIMAGENES: The poor child is trembling on account of what you're making her do.

MADAM SORBIN: You've explained why, it's because she's only a child: take heart, my daughter, express yourself clearly and speak up

LINA: My dear mother, my opinion is that, as you have said, we should be ladies and our own mistresses on an equal footing with these gentlemen; that we should work with them on framing the laws, and then we should draw what they call lots to see which one of us will become king or queen; if it's not to be that way, let everyone leave to one side or the other, we to the right, the men to the left, to the best of our abilities. Did I get it all, my mother?

MADAM SORBIN: Aren't you forgetting the clause on sweethearts?

LINA: That's because it's the hardest one to remember; your opinion still holds that love is no better than sheer idiocy.

MADAM SORBIN: You're not being asked to give my opinion, but your own.

LINA: Dear me! Mine would be to bring my sweetheart and his love along with us.

PERSINET: There you have goodness of heart, and a beautiful loving disposition.

LINA: Yes, but I've been ordered to bid you a farewell that will last for all eternity.

PERSINET: Mercy upon me!

MR. SORBIN: May heaven help us; is that a regimen for living, our wife?

MADAM SORBIN: All right, Lina, make your final curtsy to Mr. Sorbin, whom we no longer know, and let us withdraw without once looking back.

(*The women go off.*)

PERSINET: Their departure seals my death warrant, I shall never last until supper time.

HERMOCRATES: I believe you feel the urge to cry, Mr. Sorbin?

MR. SORBIN: I'm further along than that, lord Hermocrates, I'm indulging the urge.

PERSINET: If you want to see beautiful ʻears of ample dimension, you have only to look at mine.

MR. SORBIN: I love those extravagant creatures more than I thought; we would have to fight, and that's not my usual way of doing things.

TIMAGENES: I forgive your softheartedness.

PERSINET: Who does not love the fair sex?

HERMOCRATES: Leave us, little man.

PERSINET: You are the most adamant of the lot, lord Hermocrates; because here's Mr. Sorbin who is a fine example of a man; here I am grieving my heart out; here's lord Timagenes who's ready to concede; no one here is a tiger, you're the only one who's showing his claws, and if it weren't for you, we'd be sharing the farm.

HERMOCRATES: Wait, Gentlemen, we'll reach an accommodation, if that's what you want, since violent solutions are not to your liking; but I've got an idea, are you willing to put yourselves in my hands?

TIMAGENES: Agreed, act for us, we give you our powers.

MR. SORBIN: And even my office along with, if I'm permitted to hand it over.

HERMOCRATES: Run, Persinet, call them back, hurry, they can't have gone far.

PERSINET: Oh, my goodness, I'll go like the wind, I'll leap like a mountain goat.

HERMOCRATES: Also see to it that you bring me here right away a small table and something to write with.

PERSINET: This very instant. (*Exit Persinet.*)

TIMAGENES: Do you want us to withdraw?

HERMOCRATES: Yes, but since we are at war with the savages inhabiting this island, you are both to come back in a few moments and tell us that they have been seen coming down from their mountains in great numbers and are on their way here to attack us, nothing except that. You can also bring with you several men bearing arms, which you will present to the women for the battle.

(*Persinet comes back with a table, on which there is ink, paper, and a pen.*)

PERSINET: (*Setting the table down.*) Those lovely creatures are following me, and this is for your documents, Mr. Notary; try to write up the paper for us on this paper.

TIMAGENES: Let's be on our way. (*Exit Timagenes, Mr. Sorbin, and Persinet.*)

(*Enter Arthenice and Madam Sorbin.*)

HERMOCRATES: (*To Arthenice.*) You have prevailed, Madam, you triumph over a resistance that would deprive us of the happiness of living with you, and that would not have lasted long if all the women of the colony were comparable to the noble Arthenice; her reason, her refinement, her graces and her birth would have won us over in no time, but to speak frankly with you, the character of Madam Sorbin, who will share the power with you to make the laws, held us back at first. Not that we do not consider her a woman of merit in her own way, but the humbleness of her social station, which usually brings with it a certain uncouthness, the men say . . .

MADAM SORBIN: Good grief! This humble character and her humble social station . . .

HERMOCRATES: I'm not the one who says that, I'm simply telling you what they've been thinking; they even go so far as to suggest that Arthenice, refined as she is, must have a good deal of difficulty putting up with you.

ARTHENICE: (*Aside to Hermocrates.*) I advise you not to irritate her.

HERMOCRATES: As for me, I accuse you of nothing and I confine myself to telling you on behalf of those gentlemen that you will have a part in all the offices of government, and that I am ordered to draw up the deed in your presence; but before I begin, see if you have something more specific to request.

ARTHENICE: I shall not insist on anything except one clause.

MADAM SORBIN: And the same goes for me; there's one article not to my liking, and that I revoke, that's the nobility, I do away with it to get rid of humble social stations; let's not have any more of that nonsense.

ARTHENICE: What, Madam Sorbin, you're eliminating the nobles?

HERMOCRATES: I rather like that elimination.

ARTHENICE: You, Hermocrates?

HERMOCRATES: Forgive me, Madam, I have two little reasons for that, I am from the middle class and a liberal philosopher.

MADAM SORBIN: Your two reasons will find satisfaction; I order, by virtue of my plenary powers, that people named Arthenice and Sorbin be considered equal, and that it be as fine to be called Hermocrates or Fiddlesticks as Timagenes; what are names that they should be the source of fame and glory?

HERMOCRATES: Truly, she reasons like Socrates; yield to her, Madam, I am about to write it down.

ARTHENICE: I will never consent to it; I was born with an advantage that I intend to keep, if you please, Madam Handicraft.

MADAM SORBIN: Oh, come now, comrade, you have too much intelligence to be a stuck-up snob.

ARTHENICE: Try answering the accusation made against you of uncouthness!

MADAM SORBIN: Hold your tongue now, in my opinion you're like a child crying for its rattle.

HERMOCRATES: Be calm, Ladies, let's leave that article in dispute for the time being, we'll come back to it later.

MADAM SORBIN: Tell us your clause, Madam elected representative and noblewoman.

ARTHENICE: It's a bit more sensible that yours, "the Sorbin woman"; it concerns love and marriage; every single infidelity dishonors a woman; I want the male sex treated in the same way.

MADAM SORBIN: No, that's good for nothing, and I oppose it.

ARTHENICE: What I'm saying is good for nothing?

MADAM SORBIN: Nothing whatsoever, less than nothing.

HERMOCRATES: I'm not of your opinion on that matter, Madam Sorbin; I find the proposal fair, even though I'm a man.

MADAM SORBIN: I say no to it; men don't have our strength, I feel for their weakness, society has given them free rein in matters of fidelity and I leave them their freedom. How could it be otherwise? As for how it should be with us women, we are not even disgraced enough for infidelity, I call for a still stiffer dose; the harsher it is, the more honorable we shall be and the more the grandeur of our virtue will be acknowledged.

ARTHENICE: She's raving!

MADAM SORBIN: Of course, I'm speaking as a woman of humble station. You see, we women of the people don't go around changing lovers or husbands, while it's not the same with the great ladies, they don't care about moral principles and act just like men; but my regulation will keep them in line.

HERMOCRATES: What do you say to her, Madam, and what should I write?

ARTHENICE: Oh! How could I enact anything with that fishwife?

(Enter Timagenes, Mr. Sorbin, and Several Men bearing arms.)

TIMAGENES: (*To Arthenice.*) Madam, we have just sighted a vast horde of savages coming down into the plain to attack us; we have already gathered the men together; make haste on your side to assemble the women, and lead us today along with Madam Sorbin, as you begin to perform your military functions; here are some weapons that we bring you.

MADAM SORBIN: I appoint you colonel for the engagement. The men will continue as military commanders until we learn the profession of arms.

MR. SORBIN: But at least come join the battle.

ARTHENICE: That woman's crudeness disgusts me with the whole thing, and I renounce as impractical any idea of working with her.

MADAM SORBIN: Her foolish pride and vanity reconciles me with you men. Come, my husband, I forgive you; go fight, I'm going to attend to our housekeeping.

TIMAGENES: I am overjoyed to see the matter settled. Don't be alarmed, Ladies; go shelter yourselves from the war, we shall look after your rights in the customs that we are going to establish.

END

THE TWO DOUBLES

or

THE SURPRISING SURPRISE

A Parade

Thomas Simon Gueullette

CHARACTERS:

Cassander, Isabelle's husband
Isabelle, Cassander's wife

CASSANDER: (*Alone.*) I must admit that backbiting has a scandalously long tongue. A year has passed since I married the charming Isabelle; when we got married, they came at me from all sides with a hundred different stories, and among other things they told me, "Listen, old boy, you'll be sitting pretty with that girl, you'll have it made with her." But those scandal-mongers have been shown up, because since the day I married her, I never could, despite all my efforts and the various techniques I brought to bear, succeed in robbing her of the flower of her chastity, and not having done so, I think I can boast that my wife has never besmirched her virtue, not even with me. But on second thought, I'm suffering on account of these impregnable obstacles, and besides Isabelle, being so young, puts me to perpetual tests which I cannot pass. So on the sly I've begun getting chummy with the beautiful Floozie, who lives near us. Floozie has reached a ripe age, she's a girl who's been around a bit, and with her I'm sure to find such a warm welcome that one way or the other I'll end up enjoying the most perfect bliss. But I'm afraid that my wife will pay me back tit for tat. I've been warned that my old pal Leander has been trying to get his hand in. Since that's what I've got to find out, I'm going to borrow Leander's Sunday best, and making use of that disguise, I'll talk love to my wife to see if she'll respond favorably. Now I have to say goodbye to her in order to deceive her better. Isabelle . . . Isabelle . . . (*Enter Isabelle.*)

ISABELLE: Whatcha want, dear husband of mine?

CASSANDER: Come here, closer, little doggie of my soul, sugar candy of my love, liquorice stick of my pleasures.

ISABELLE: That's a good one! How is that possible! You always find excuses

. for what puts your nose out of joint.

CASSANDER: Now, now, my Seraphina, it'll come back one of these days. As my hair grows whiter and whiter, I can feel my love for you grow and stretch.

ISABELLE: Sure, soon it will be dragging along the floor.

CASSANDER: Kiss me, my little chickie, stick out your roguish little snout, g-g-g-give your house sparrow a beakful.

ISABELLE: That birdie isn't black-throated.

CASSANDER: I'm paying you all these cute little compliments, my pretty, only to console you in advance for the disagreeably annoying news I must announce to you, I am painfully obliged, by a necessarily essential obligation, to leave you all alone this afternoon.

ISABELLE: What a pity! It will be exactly the same as when you're here. I'll keep busy all by myself waiting for you; you know I'm one of those women who like to keep their ten fingers going.

CASSANDER: There, there, don't tell lies, you'll lose; because we would have played a hundred little games.

ISABELLE: That's a good one! A lot I ever win; when we play, you never put anything up.

CASSANDER: I'll put something up, I'll put something up if treated with patience.

ISABELLE: Oh, I've never worn anyone's patience thin.

CASSANDER: Goodbye, goodbye, my precious, until we meet again.

ISABELLE: Then you won't be coming back to spend the night?

CASSANDER: Good grief! No danger of my doing you that wrong, dearest rascal. You know perfectly well that I don't spend the night out.

ISABELLE: (Aside.) But you don't spend it in either.

CASSANDER: Goodbye again, little baby, think only about having a good time and laughing all by yourself while I'm gone. (Exit.)

ISABELLE: (Alone.) Get along with you, get along with you, nasty doddering lech, dirty old goat, senile cuckold, a lot I care for your advice! I must admit I'm in a terrible fix, I've never been wilder since I first turned woman. It's a terrible torment to be involved with a man who's only got a wagging tongue and yet who's still always chasing after you. I'd prefer to be paid off and sent on my way; I'd be better off not being married. You see, I'd as soon have my bowl empty as have nothing in it. So I've made up my mind; and since Mister Leander has written me a letter declaring his love, I want to see what tune he's singing, and if he has as much to offer as he says he has. After all, a respectable woman has the right to seek compensation for the misery her husband causes her by seizing the transitory pleasures of life in the solace of happy days. More than once now we would have taken the necessary steps if I hadn't needed a pretext to have lovers. I'm sure that fortune favors me with the opportunity, and that my ugly old ape vacated the premises to visit Mademoiselle Floozie, our neighbor. I'm going to disguise myself as her, he'll mistake me for our neighborhood Floozie; if he takes any liberties with me, I'll make his crest fall by disclosing who I am, and then he won't dare say anything when I decide to kick my heels up higher than my ass. (*Exit.*)

CASSANDER: (*Alone.*) Now I'm perfectly disguised, and my old pal Leander, whose only suit is his Sunday best, lent it to me; it fits me like two peas in a pod; and what is most particularly extraordinary is that with these new clothes on, I feel re-invigorated with a charge of new vigor. All right, that's all to the good, provided it lasts. Youth is a precious thing, and what's always troubled me is that you're no longer young once you've grown old. Where are the days when I used to say to a beauty, "My divinity, is it really true that you've never yet loved anyone?" They'd tell me, "You'll see, sir," and they did their utmost to convince me by the most sensuous of evidence. Where are the days, when with a generous sense of enterprise, I did not allow any part of the globe to escape my vigorous curiosity, and when I ordered a consignment of Negresses from the depths of America for my exclusive use. Be that as it may, let's not say another word on the subject, but think only how to test my wife.

(*Enter Isabelle as Floozie.*)

ISABELLE: (*Aside.*) I think that in these clothes I look quite a bit like Floozie; just let my husband come. But what's this I see? Isn't that my dear Leander? Yes, I'm sure it is, because those are his clothes and that's his wig. How well dressed he is! How elegant! I'm sure it's to dazzle me.

CASSANDER: (*As Leander; aside.*) Yes, it's her, it's my Floozie; while I'm waiting to go find my wife, I must pay her a small compliment. Appearing as Leander won't make her forget the affection she promised she'd show me.

ISABELLE: (*Aside.*) Leander doesn't recognize me, he takes me for Floozie. Let's see if he's capable of being true, and of refusing a girl who asks him to respond lovingly to her affection.

CASSANDER: Charming Floozie, you see before you Mister Leander who comes to put his heart in your feet, and whose flame burns endlessly without the power to extinguish the ardor he has to be your humble servant.

ISABELLE: Sir, for a long time now I have been hoping that you would say a few words to me about it, and I am glad that you find me the boot that fits your foot.

CASSANDER: When a person is as beautiful as you are, Mamselle, a person must not be astonished if that person suits everyone's taste; and you are much too charming not to be a saddle for all horses. But, Mamselle, as I am a young man of rank and social standing, I beg you to have the goodness not to keep my love chafing at the bit, because I've got a lot of other things to do.

ISABELLE: Sir, I realize that a petty nobleman doesn't have too much time to spare, that's why I'll tell you right away that I love you with all my heart, in return for which I hope that you'll take into account the fact that a girl like me must be well dressed and well fed in order to love a nobleman properly.

CASSANDER: Mamselle, I'm able to give you a taffeta dress and a turkey in response to your requirement, so let that be no obstacle.

ISABELLE: As part of the bargain, I'd like to have you stop fooling around with that stuck-up old bat, Mamselle Isabelle, to whom you've been writing love letters.

CASSANDER: (*Under his breath.*) My wife gets letters from Leander, and Floozie, no more than she, doesn't give a damn for my love. Sssh, not a word. (*Aloud.*) No sooner said than done, Mamselle, and I promise you I'll give Isabelle a few swift kicks in the backside, with all undue deference to you.

ISABELLE: (*Under her breath.*) Oh, that miserable traitor Leander!

CASSANDER: But on condition that you kick out that old duffer Cassander, to whom you've already shown some small favors.

ISABELLE: (*Under her breath.*) So it's true my decrepit old husband has been going into town to get his hopes up. Not another word. (*Aloud.*) Can you believe that I'd let myself go with a dislocated old carcass like him? Rest assured in the certainty of my love.

CASSANDER: Then will you always love Leander?

ISABELLE: Until the moment when the termination of my life has ended, provided that you always love Floozie.

CASSANDER: Until death in the tomb?

(*Cassander and Isabelle exclaim at the same time:*)

ISABELLE: Oh, faithless Leander, do you know who I am?

CASSANDER: Oh, treacherous Floozie, do you recognize Leander?

ISABELLE: My husband!

CASSANDER: My wife!

ISABELLE: Well then, my husband, you think you're with Floozie.

CASSANDER: Well then, Madam my wife, you thought you were with Leander.

ISABELLE: (*Giving him a slap.*) For Leander, there, that's for you.

CASSANDER: (*Giving her a kick in the ass.*) For Floozie, there, give her that.

ISABELLE: (*Giving him a punch.*) There, put that in his chapel.

CASSANDER: (*Giving her a slap.*) There, hang that up in her pew and sprinkle holy water on it.

ISABELLE: (*Pulling off his wig.*) There, send him that by mail.

CASSANDER: (*Pulling off her head-dress.*) That's to pay the postage with.

ISABELLE: Dirty dog, bad breath, runny nose, broken-down old wagon.

CASSANDER: Old fox, hag, death mask, double trouble.

ISABELLE: So you think I didn't recognize you, nasty old cuckold?

CASSANDER: (*Mellowing.*) What, you knew it was your husband? I'd like to think so, because I for my part knew perfectly well that you were my dear wife.

ISABELLE: Is it true, dear husband of mine, that we did what we did for laughs?

CASSANDER: Take my word as a man of honor, I think we did. Let's kiss and make up.

ISABELLE: Gladly, my dear spouse: in any case, you'd be making a big mistake to look elsewhere for opportunities, because I can assure you that an Isabelle and a Floozie are one and the same.

CASSANDER: Absolutely the same. That's right, my child, and you can count on the fact that the most handsome Leander is often nothing but an out-and-out old duffer Cassander. Let's head for the house, my girl, and gear all our efforts to effecting a much closer reconciliation.

END

A PARADE (Directoire Period)

A PARADE (Théâtres des Boulevards)

THE BLIND
ONE-ARMED DEAF-MUTE

A Parade

Thomas Simon Gueullette

CHARACTERS:

The Master
Giles
The Sharper

MASTER: Hey there, Giles! Hey! I always have to shout myself hoarse when I want that rascal. Giles, Giles.

GILES: (*Comes up to him without making a sound and speaks very loudly in his ear.*) Here I am, sir.

MASTER: Confound that rascal! Does he want to frighten me to death.

GILES: Why, sir, you were shouting like a stick that had lost its blind man.

MASTER: And why don't you come when you're called?

GILES: Sir, everyone has things to do; I was in circumference with the post-man: he just brought me a letter, and I was asking him to read it to me when you called me.

MASTER: Did he read it to you?

GILES: You didn't give me time.

MASTER: Where does this letter come from?

GILES: I don't know, I'm telling you, I barely had time to unseal it.

MASTER: Let's see.

GILES: Here you are, sir, here it is.

MASTER: (*Reads.*) From the country . . . Where in the country?

GILES: From Limoges, I guess.

MASTER: Then it should say so.

GILES: Oh, we're not all that smart in Limoges; keep on reading, please.

MASTER: (*Reads.*) "My Cousin Giles, this is to advise you that my aunt, your mother, is dead."

GILES: (*Weeping.*) My mother is dead! Oh, sir, then I'm an orphan. Who will take care of me now?

MASTER: Look here, you're big enough to be your own mother and father;

I'm delighted to see you show such strong feelings of attachment to your mother, but we are all mortal, let's go on with the letter. (*He reads.*) "She has left you fifty crowns."

GILES: My mother's left me fifty crowns? Now that's what I call a good woman. Sir, is that point quite sure?

MASTER: That's what's written here. But it seems to me that you're quickly consoled for the loss of your mother?

GILES: Oh, she was really old!

MASTER: Well, if that's the case. (*He reads.*) "I hasten to inform you that your little sister Floozie has become a prostitute . . ."

GILES: My sister Floozie a prostitute! (*He weeps.*) Sir, I'll beat that hussy to a pulp; I love honor a hundred times more than a good name.

MASTER: There, there, be comforted.

GILES: No, sir, I won't do anything of the sort.

MASTER: Listen. (*He reads.*) "In four months of leading a dissolute life, she saved up six hundred pounds."

GILES: (*Begins to laugh.*) Six hundred pounds! That's pretty good; say, my sister Floozie was thrifty, and apparently she got paid well.

MASTER: So it seems. (*He reads.*) "I must tell you, Cousin, that during a quarrel two weeks ago with a sword-wielding brawler, she got slashed in the face and it left her horribly disfigured.

GILES: (*Weeping.*) Oh! Poor little Floozie, how I pity you: now she won't be able to do her job half as well as before. What a shame! That's what happens to almost all girls like her.

MASTER: Wait, my friend. (*He reads.*) "As the wound was dangerous, she made her will, and you figure prominently in it."

GILES: What a good heart that girl has!

MASTER: (*Reads.*) "Soon afterwards she died."

GILES: Oh, sir, my heart is breaking.

MASTER: (*Reads.*) "According to her will she leaves you a sumptuously furnished house."

GILES: (*Laughing very loudly.*) A sumptuously furnished house! Now that was really nice of her. By golly, she's a good creature, and a truly decent girl.

MASTER: A decent girl!

GILES: Sure she is, at least toward me, now I'm really rich. Fifty crowns from my mother, and a furnished house from my sister.

MASTER: No more need to pity the poor orphan, eh, Giles?

GILES: I should say not, the orphan is pretty pleased. Let's hear the rest, maybe there's sumpin' else good for me in it.

MASTER: (*Reads.*) Let's see. "But, my dear Cousin, a terrible disaster occurred quite unexpectedly. The house caught fire and burned down, and all the furniture was destroyed; what was not consumed by the flames was pillaged by looters, and your fifty crowns were stolen."

GILES: Fire! Stop thieves! Oh, sir, I'm ruined, quickly, write to them in the country and tell them to use all the buckets in town and have them throw as much water as possible on the fire.

MASTER: Look here, my poor Giles, your head's starting to spin. Before the letter could get there, the fire would have destroyed the whole town.

GILES: Oh, sir, now that does it! I don't want to go on living after such a disaster: my mother's dead, my poor sister Floozie's passed away, I have no reason to go on living either.

MASTER: Come, come, Giles, be brave, let's go inside; come have a drink, then I'll have you go deliver some money—thirty gold pistoles—to my lawyer.

GILES: Oh, sir, I don't have the strength.

(The Master takes Giles off.)

SHARPER: *(Entering.)* Mister Bejabbers's decision really makes me happy; if he's gullible enough to hand over the thirty pistoles he was talking about to his valet Giles, it won't be long before I get my hands on that money; in fact, I've got a soldier's uniform ready near-by; that's all I need to do the job. *(Exit.)*

MASTER: *(Re-entering.)* I feel sorry for that poor unhappy Giles, he's crying his eyes out; but it's less for his mother and sister than for the inheritance he was counting on. Several glasses of wine will make him forget his sorrow: but I see him coming. *(Enter Giles.)* Come now, my friend, cheer up, you're letting yourself be discouraged for nothing.

GILES: Oh, sir, it's all over now, and I've made up my mind.

MASTER: What do you mean, you've made up your mind?

GILES: Sir, it means that since I love you, I want to die in your arms.

MASTER: Die, in my arms!

GILES: Yes, sir, I have less than two hours left to live.

MASTER: But, my friend, you're crazy.

GILES: No, sir, I've just taken poison.

MASTER: Merciful heavens!

GILES: Yes, sir, you remember last year someone sent you six white earthenware jars that I thought were preserves.

MASTER: Yes, I remember all that.

GILES: Well, then, sir, so as to join my mother and my little sister Floozie, I've just swallowed what was in two of those jars.

MASTER: Oh, you wretch, it was apple jelly.

GILES: I knew that's what it was, sir, and it's not a disagreeable poison to take: but I can tell that it's already taking effect. Oh, sir, I'm dying . . .

MASTER: Oh, good heavens! Is it possible?

GILES: Don't make me go all soft, sir, I beg you, hear my final farewells.

MASTER: Your final farewells!

GILES: Yes, sir, give my regards to Jacqueline.

MASTER: Look! You're a raving idiot.

GILES: Oh, sir, it's inhuman to treat me that way, I'm burning up . . .

MASTER: I can well believe it, I really can, to gulp down two whole jars of preserves all at once.

GILES: Poisoned jam, that's the hell of it: hold me up, sir; farewell my dear master; you're losing a valet who is very fond of you.

MASTER: I must admit I've been duped by that beast. I know his weakness for food; to keep him from eating my preserves, I made him think it was poison, while all the time it was perfectly good apple jelly from Normandy, and that fool goes and eats two jars of it thinking he's killing himself.

GILES: What, sir, it wasn't poison?

MASTER: No, you dolt, and if you have no other reason to fear death, you can set your mind at rest, and I got off a lot cheaper than I might have.

GILES: Yes indeed, I've seen death from close up; but since you tell me I won't die of it, long live Giles, I don't regret I swallowed that stuff because I found the poison very sweet.

MASTER: I can well believe it, but now that you've been reassured, will you have enough presence of mind to bring my lawyer, Mister Lightfingers, the thirty gold pistoles that are in this purse?

GILES: Oh, sir, you can count on my trustworthiness.

MASTER: It's not your trustworthiness I have doubts about, it's your doltishness that makes me afraid someone will trick you out of those thirty pistoles.

GILES: Depend on me, sir, have no fears.

MASTER: All right, here are the thirty pistoles in this purse. While you go deliver the money, I'll take a turn round the ramparts. (*Exit.*)

GILES: By gosh, if I ever thought I was going to die, it was then. But it was my master's fault; just what did he have in mind when he told me it was poison? But who is that odd-looking fish after?

SHARPER: (*Entering.*) My lord, have pity on a poor gentleman who is reduced to extreme poverty and yet who cannot beg for his living.

GILES: And why, my friend, can't you beg for your living?

SHARPER: Because, my lord, I've been mute for three years.

GILES: You've been mute for three years?

SHARPER: That's right, my lord.

GILES: And how did that happen to you? Did you have an accident?

SHARPER: It was when, to keep myself amused, I was carrying a hod in a building where I worked as a laborer; a rung on the ladder having broken under me, I hit my chin on a rung higher up, and that cut my tongue right off.

GILES: You got your tongue cut off?

SHARPER: Yes, sir, see, this is all I've got left.

GILES: Well, I'll be! You must have had a very long one to start with?

SHARPER: Yes, sir, people always told me I had a long tongue.

GILES: And just how much do you still have left?

SHARPER: About this much.

GILES: Well, now, that's not at all bad for a hodcarrier, and since then you haven't been able to speak any more?

SHARPER: No, sir.

GILES: And then just what are you doing now?

SHARPER: Nothing, sir.

GILES: What do you mean nothing? You've been talking a blue streak.

SHARPER: Oh, sir, I haven't opened my mouth.

GILES: But you've been talking with me for a quarter of an hour.

SHARPER: Well, yes, that's true, but only to beg for the bare necessities.

GILES: But that's still talking.

SHARPER: I better explain it all to you. What happened was that a clever quack got hold of me, and promised to cure me, but only so I could beg for my living: he told me he couldn't do any more for me, and that I'd have to wait three months for the operation to take place.

GILES: And how many of his cures did you take?

SHARPER: Who do you take me for, sir? I didn't take any of his cures.

GILES: You didn't take any?

SHARPER: No, sir, he gave them to me.

GILES: It comes to the same thing.

SHARPER: In that case, sir, it must have lasted about twelve weeks.

GILES: And how many months does that make?

SHARPER: I think it makes three.

GILES: Oh, then I'm not surprised any more at what happened; it was those drugs that gave you back the use of your speech.

SHARPER: So you think I'm speaking, sir?

GILES: If I think it's so, it's certain; you're speaking and you're speaking very distinctly.

SHARPER: Well, so much the better, sir, I'm very glad. (*He weeps.*)

GILES: You're very glad, and yet you're weeping, what does that mean?

SHARPER: It's because while the quack was busy curing me, I forgot to ask him to cure my eyesight.

GILES: Do you have bad eyesight?

SHAPER: Oh, it couldn't be worse, sir, I'm blind.

GILES: Blind! That's not possible.

SHARPER: It's only too true, sir, and once again it happened to me because of an odd and comical accident.

GILES: How about telling me what happened?

SHARPER: Here's the story in brief, sir. A big fat girl who lived in our village had a lachrymal fistula on her behind. Someone had to take a thick straw tube and blow a corrosive powder into the sore. No one wanted to under-take this assignment, for fear of swallowing that burning powder while breathing: I accepted the job out of sheer kindheartedness, in return for a six-pound crown. I blew the powder; but the girl who started to laugh just as the operation got underway let go a terrible fart and sent half that powder right in my eyes, and I instantly lost my sight.

GILES: You know, that really is a very unusual occurrence; so since that time you don't see clearly any more?

SHARPER: No, sir.

GILES: I'm going to see if he's tricking me. Fortunately I've got on me an eighty-sou coin and several liards. Here, my friend. (*He offers him in one hand the eighty sous and in the other a liard, worth only a quarter of a sou; the Sharper examines the two coins and takes the eighty sous.*)

SHARPER: I thank you, sir.

GILES: But you took the eighty-sou coin, didn't you?

SHARPER: Yes, sir, I saw that it was more valuable than the liard. That's the only faculty of eyesight I have left.

GILES: You look just like a cheat and a swindler to me.

SHARPER: Oh, sir, it's wrong of you to insult me, and you're really lucky that I'm deaf, because if I'd heard what you just said . . .

GILES: What was it?

SHARPER: That I look like a cheat and a swindler!

GILES: You heard that? Then you're not deaf?

SHARPER: Excuse me, sir, I don't hear anything except when people call me names, so watch out, my friend.

GILES: That certainly is miraculous.

SHARPER: That's true, but all of that would be nothing if I had the use of my left arm that's all shriveled, and if a cannon-ball hadn't torn off my other arm.

GILES: But it seems to me he makes quite good use of his left arm. (*Giles offers him money, and the Sharper reaches out his arm.*) You still reach out your arm pretty well.

SHARPER: Yes, sir, when I'm offered something.

GILES: And where did you lose your other arm?

SHARPER: At Port Mahon.

GILES: Did you have that uniform on then?

SHARPER: Yes, sir, it's my uniform as an orderly.

GILES: (*Aside.*) I've got you this time. (*Aloud.*) But how did the cannon-ball tear off your arm and leave the sleeve?

SHARPER: (*Aside.*) I'm caught like a real blockhead . . . (*Aloud.*) Sir, haven't you ever heard how lightning can melt a sword in its scabbard, without damaging the scabbard?

GILES: No.

SHARPER: That's a known fact. Well then, this is almost exactly the same thing: the cannon-ball went through the pores of the sleeve on my jacket.

GILES: Without damaging it?

SHARPER: That's right, sir.

GILES: Gee whiz, that's really astonishing! Let me examine that sleeve a little bit.

SHARPER: You can see for yourself, sir. (*During the examination, the Sharper picks Giles's pocket until Giles finally grabs his hand.*)

GILES: Oh, Mister Swindler, you say that you lost your arm, and here it is.

SHARPER: What's that, sir?

GILES: Your arm.

SHARPER: My arm, that's not possible.

GILES: I'm holding on to it.

SHARPER: You're holding on to it! Oh, sir, I'm much obliged to you!

GILES: Don't mention it.

SHARPER: That cheat of a surgeon who dressed my wound for three months, trying to make me believe I'd lost it! But it turns out he was a terrible scoundrel!

GILES: You're playing dumb, but I don't intend to be taken in by you.

SHARPER: Oh, I'm being perfectly sincere, and I'm much obliged to you for having found my arm for me.

GILES: I'm not swallowing that story, you're a cheat, I tell you . . . a thief . . .

SHARPER: A cheat? You're the one who's a cheat.

GILES: Me?

SHARPER: Yes, a cheat and a thief; you stole my arm and my hand.

GILES: Now that's really going too far.

SHARPER: Wasn't my hand in your pocket?

GILES: Yes, by George, it certainly was.

SHARPER: Isn't the hand connected to the arm?

GILES: It sure is.

SHARPER: Well then, you're the one who put my hand in your pocket and who hid it from me, along with my arm, for such a long time. I'm going to lodge a complaint, and I'll have you hanged, do you understand?

GILES: Holy Moses, this is getting serious.

SHARPER: Very serious indeed. Close on the heels of the army there's always a huge band of swindlers like you, who steal our arms and legs when we're not looking: our General had a dozen of them strung up during the last campaign, and you look to me exactly like the person who'll be the thirteenth today. Come on, off to prison with you.

GILES: To prison?

SHARPER: Yes, to prison, and in twenty-four hours it'll be all over with you.

GILES: But I can prove I never was in Berg-op-zoom.

SHARPER: But I'll come up with twenty witnesses who'll swear that you were. Come on, off you go to prison.

GILES: Wait a minute now! Isn't there any way we could settle this business just between the two of us?

SHARPER: How could we settle it? Since the last campaign when you stole my arm from me, I haven't been able to work, and I would have earned more than fifty pistoles.

GILES: Well now, as for fifty pistoles, I don't have that much, but there are thirty pistoles in this purse I was going to bring my Master's lawyer. Would you be satisfied with that amount?

SHARPER: It's very little, and I'll be taking a loss, but I'm not a bad sort, and I'm willing to settle for such a modest sum: but don't ever do that again: damn it all, an arm stolen that way can have very grave consequences.

GILES: I can certainly believe that, but to tell the truth, it wasn't me who took your arm.

SHARPER: Then how did it get into your pocket?

GILES: I swear, I don't have any idea.

SHARPER: So long, until we meet again: the first time that our paths cross again, I'll buy the bottle.

GILES: (*Alone.*) With pleasure. Good gosh, I'm still lucky to get off so easy. Our Master can get as angry as he likes, but I still prefer to give away his thirty pistoles than to get thrown into prison.

(*The Master returns from his walk; he asks Giles if he found his lawyer, Giles tells him what just happened to him, gets all mixed up in his story, makes his Master lose his temper until finally his Master beats him and drives him offstage. This ends the parade.*)

END

THE SHIT MERCHANT

A Parade

Thomas Simon Gueullette

CHARACTERS:

Leander
Harlequin
Giles
Floozie
Apothecary

LEANDER: Listen, my dear Harlequin.

HARLEQUIN: Sure I will, Sir, I'm not deaf.

LEANDER: Always ready with a joke as usual, but that's not what we're concerned with now. I've always told you my griefs and misfortunes.

HARLEQUIN: That's right, Sir.

LEANDER: I've got a grievance, my dear Harlequin. It's certainly not against the charming Zusabelle. Never could a girl be more polite or refined, she loves me every day; but then you know perfectly well that I go spend the night at her house ordinarily.

HARLEQUIN: That's right, Sir.

LEANDER: And I don't bear any grudge against fortune; thank Heavens, I've always got a silver coin to buy a bottle of wine for a friend.

HARLEQUIN: I'd like to have one of those coins to buy a roast chicken with and a dozen bottles of wine.

LEANDER: When will you ever become more unassuming, my dear Harlequin; won't the good example of the fine manners you can observe in me make you mend your ways?

HARLEQUIN: But, Sir, you know what they say: like man, like Master.

LEANDER: That's true, that's what everyone says.

HARLEQUIN: You've got a mistress, you've got a silver coin; if I had only a quarter of a mistress, and two silver coins, I'd be happier than the Pope.

LEANDER: Quiet, insolent wretch, you're not to talk of such people; but I promise you the wherewithal to have a good bottle of full-bodied wine, if you take an interest in my misfortune.

HARLEQUIN: Talk fast, I'm dying of thirst.

LEANDER: You know that rascally lout of a Giles who lives near-by?

HARLEQUIN: Do I know him! Haven't I stared him down a hundred times!

LEANDER: Well, he's a filthy beast who comes every day (words don't stink) to drop his excrement, his dirty business on my doorstep.

HARLEQUIN: And for that you're going to give me a bottle of wine?

LEANDER: You're always in such a state of impetuosity . . .

HARLEQUIN: If you want me to do the same thing on his doorstep, you have only to say so, it'll be done right away, that'll be money well earned.

LEANDER: No, I tell you.

HARLEQUIN: Look, you're making my mouth water.

LEANDER: Will you listen to me.

HARLEQUIN: If that's all it takes to oblige a friend, I'll dish it out in generous portions.

LEANDER: Will you shut up?

HARLEQUIN: You're the one who got me going.

LEANDER: What again!

HARLEQUIN: Don't get angry, Sir, but hurry up, I'm in a rush.

LEANDER: I'd like to punish that insolent wretch who has the audacity . . .

HARLEQUIN: To shit on our doorstep.

LEANDER: But how could such a thing happen? Is it possible! Just because I gave him a few good beatings.

HARLEQUIN: If that's the way it went, I'd've shit in your bed, that's what I'd've done. But, Sir, don't you worry, I promise you I'll avenge you. Look, there he is, coming out of the house, let's go back in. You're going to see me outwit him, I've just had an idea that's not half bad.

LEANDER: You see, my dear Harlequin, your Master confides in you all his grievances.

HARLEQUIN: All right, I tell you, we're going to outwit him. (*Exit Harlequin and Leander.*)

GILES: (*Alone.*) Ever since I lost my Unk, I'm bored at home, I don't know what to do with my ten fingers; after all, you can't sit around and scratch yourself all the time; I've got to get married; my wife will scratch me, I'll scratch her, we'll scratch each other; I'll beat her, she'll beat me, we'll beat each other, and then we'll make up, and then . . . By gosh, there she is; speak of the devil, and he is sure to appear. I sure wish she'd speak of me. (*Enter Floozie.*)

GILES: (*Circling around Floozie.*) By golly, that's what you call a good household ass, a good . . .

FLOOZIE: What are you looking at there, Mister Giles?

GILES: I was giving you the once-over, Mamselle; and what are you doing like that all by yourself?

FLOOZIE: I know what you've got in mind, joker; but to get married, you have to have the wherewithal, and I don't have what it takes to buy a halfpint of wine, or even a cup of Swiss coffee.

GILES: So much the better, I don't either.

FLOOZIE: So much the worse, and what about dipping into the pot?

GILES: We won't be doing that, any little thing makes it run over. All right, all right, it doesn't matter, look at me, I've got all my arms and legs, I'll find the wherewithal; if only people with independent incomes committed follies, there wouldn't be so many cuckolds.

FLOOZIE: All that is well and good, Mister Giles, but you've got to have ready cash.

GILES: Oh, Mamselle, you've got enough for the two of us, but by golly, I'm really glad to see you before things go much further.

FLOOZIE: Why's that?

GILES: Trot, walk, strut your stuff for me.

FLOOZIE: Like that, Mister Giles?

GILES: Yes, that's it, I don't want to buy a pig in a poke; but tell me something?

FLOOZIE: What?

GILES: Are you really a maiden all over?

FLOOZIE: Oh, almost everywhere. Rest assured that I'm as much of a maiden as my mother was after bringing me into the world. That's all I can say.

GILES: Oh, if that's the way it is, I have nothing more to say, because your mother certainly wasn't a man.

FLOOZIE: That's right, but Mister Giles, I'm wasting my time diddling around here. Your ass is a dumb beast riding on a donkey's back if you think you'll marry me without having anything or knowing how to earn a living. I'm your servant, Mister Giles. (*Exit Floozie.*)

GILES: (*Alone.*) By golly, she's right; I've got to figure out how to do something. Let's see now. (*He enumerates all the various professions.*) If I had an independent income, I wouldn't have so much trouble finding a profession. All right, I've got to look for one. I'll marry Floozie, I'll have lots of little children; all the girls will be Floozies, and all the boys will be Gileses. By golly, I'll have quite a family.

HARLEQUIN: (*Enters, carrying a big cask.*) Oh, good day, Giles; how are you getting along?

GILES: Not bad, no money, no worries, and what about you?

HARLEQUIN: I've gone into dealing in merchandise.

GILES: Well I'll be darned! And what are you selling?

HARLEQUIN: (*Making him smell a specimen taken from the cask.*) There, see if you can identify the merchandise.

GILES: (*Holding his nose.*) By golly, I sure can; that's something I make every day, it's shit. Can you sell it?

HARLEQUIN: I should say you can, there's even a big market for it now; where have you been?

GILES: I never heard of anything like that, and I see so much of it in the streets that no one ever touches.

HARLEQUIN: That's because there are so many people in other professions that it never occurs to them.

GILES: Sure as I'm talking to you, I don't have any profession and yet it never occurred to me either. Oh, what a lot I've wasted! But who do you sell it to?

HARLEQUIN: To all kinds of people, but especially to apothecaries. Stay right where you are, you'll see. (*Enter the Apothecary.*)

HARLEQUIN: Sir, would you like to buy my merchandise, I'll sell it cheap!

APOTHECARY: Let's have a look, Sir, let's have a look.

HARLEQUIN: Try it, Sir, examine it carefully, you won't find any better.

APOTHECARY: The merchandise could be in better shape. But let's see, the price is the big thing; how much do you want for it?

HARLEQUIN: I'm asking seven crowns.

APOTHECARY: Now look here, that's too much; will you take five?

HARLEQUIN: Oh, I can't, Sir, I'd lose too much on the deal.

GILES: (*Aside.*) He'd lose on the deal?

HARLEQUIN: Believe me, Sir, don't let me get away. I'm supplying one of your colleagues who won't haggle; perhaps he'll give me more for it.

APOTHECARY: All right then, there's your seven crowns since you refuse to come down any. (*Exit the Apothecary.*)

HARLEQUIN: Well, there, did I sell it or didn't I? And if the merchandise was going good, I'd've gotten a lot more.

GILES: By golly, that's amazing! I wouldn't have believed it if I hadn't seen it with my own eyes. All right, that decides it. I'm becoming a Shit Merchant; I was looking for a profession, this one isn't difficult, I'll be a Grand Master right off the bat, and Floozie won't have anything more to reproach me with. Mister Harlequin, I'm much obliged to you. (*Exit Giles.*)

HARLEQUIN: (*Alone, laughing.*) What a queer duck! I've given him a profession all right with which he's going to make a huge fortune, but at least our neighborhood will be clean, he'll stop shitting on our doorstep, and Mister Leander will give me a little something to buy a drink with. Here's the Apothecary who doesn't seem too happy with his merchandise, let's get out of here fast. (*Exit Harlequin.*)

APOTHECARY: If I could get my hands on that insolent wretch, that crook who sold me shit pretending it was honey, I'd make him realize an Apothecary is not someone to be made fun of. I don't dare complain about the trick he's played on me, everyone would laugh at me all over again. What can I do? I've got to be patient even though I'm fuming.

(*Enter Giles with a barrel.*)

GILES: Who wants my shit? Money for my shit; get it while it's fresh.

APOTHECARY: There's one of those crooks, or someone who's trying to ridicule me.

GILES: Oh, Sir, take advantage of the bargain, I'm forced to sell cheap.

APOTHECARY: You're an insolent wretch.

GILES: Sir, Sir, you shouldn't treat an honest Merchant the way you do.

APOTHECARY: (*Boxing his ears.*) A Merchant, my ass.

GILES: I'll bet your ass doesn't produce any as good as that. But try it before you run down the merchandise, you'll see that it's better quality than what you bought a little while ago.

APOTHECARY: (*Taking a stick.*) This rascal will pay for what that other one did.

GILES: A little while ago you paid seven crowns for a small barrel, didn't you? Well then, I'll let you have this one, which is three times bigger, for ten crowns; you should consider that something of a windfall.

APOTHECARY: (*Beating him and breaking the barrel over his body.*) There, Shit Merchant, keep your merchandise for yourself and get out of here. (*Exit the Apothecary.*)

GILES: (*Alone.*) Stop thief, stop thief, I'm a ruined man, there's no law and order here.

(*Enter Harlequin and Leander.*)

HARLEQUIN: What are you screeching about?

GILES: Oh, my dear colleague, you see how they treat Merchants.

HARLEQUIN: You better lodge a complaint with the Police Commissioner.

GILES: I'm ready to.

HARLEQUIN: Maybe you did something wrong? But, you know, it's not such a difficult profession.

GILES: No, really, I assure you, the merchandise was good; smell it if you don't believe me, you should be able to tell. That mean asshole of an Apothecary didn't even want to try it.

HARLEQUIN: Maybe he had a cold.

LEANDER: Mister Giles, we must hope you'll have better luck next time; keep trying.

GILES: By golly, Sir, I'm really fed up with the business.

LEANDER: But believe me, don't go shit on other people's doorsteps, keep your merchandise for yourself.

HARLEQUIN: We've given you a taste of your sample all over your body.

(*Enter Floozie.*)

FLOOZIE: Oh, my poor Giles, what happened to you? There's no coming near you.

GILES: You see, I wanted to set up shop so as to be able to marry you; I became a Shit Merchant.

FLOOZIE: That's what my nose tells me, blockhead. I don't want a husband who's already that much of a fool; I want to be able to make a fool of him myself. Your servant, Sir. (*She leaves.*)

LEANDER: And I don't want a neighbor who comes and shits on my doorstep every day. (*He leaves.*)

HARLEQUIN: And I don't ever want to speak to a man who's such a poor salesman of his own merchandise. (*Exit Harlequin.*)

GILES: (*Alone.*) Goodbye then. By golly, living in this world is no easy matter.

END

THE
SEVEN LEAGUE BOOTS

A Parade in One Act

Beaumarchais

CHARACTERS:

Cassander, Isabelle's father
Isabelle, Cassander's daughter, in love with Leander
Leander, Isabelle's sweetheart
Giles, Cassander's valet [his face whitened with flour]
Harlequin, Leander's valet [wears a black mask]

The action takes place near Montfaucon, opposite Mr. Cassander's house. [Then a suburb of Paris, now in the 19th arrondissement, Montfaucon was the site of a famous gallows built in the 13th century and destroyed in 1760; it was also a district known for its cattle markets and slaughterhouses.]

BARKER'S SPIEL

HARLEQUIN AND GILES: (*Coming out from two opposite sides of the stage and shouting in unison.*) The Seven League Boots, Ladies 'n Gentlemen, the Seven League Boots! Hurry! Hurry! 'Sno time to lose, we is gonna begin immejitly.

GILES: Here's where you getta see that famuss pair of fairies, and those famuss boots b'longin' to the famuss Tom Thumb, boots made so famuss throughout the entire famuss universe of the hull wide world by the famuss story wrote by the famuss author, Mister Charles Perrault, onna counta the famuss and unique power they had, 'mong many others, of growin' larger or smaller accordin' to the more'r-less famuss leg of whoever put 'em on. A power, Gentlemen, unfortunately, unknown to all the most famuss fairies, past, present, an' future.

HARLEQUIN: The title is of the rarest rarity, Ladies 'n' Gentlemen, but the show itself is even rarer. So don't go, 'cording to the fashion of judgin' the man by the clothes or the book by the kiver, and think that our parade is sumpin' to boot. That's jess the come-on, Gentlemen, that's jess the come-on. Quit that foolin' around with those ladies; getcher tickets and come on inside.

GILES: Ladies 'n' Gentlemen, you are about to beehold the on-stage appearance of that famuss Isabelle without a peer, that intimitable actress who performs comedy like she'd invented it herself in person.

HARLEQUIN: Showmen udder'n us, Gentlemen, wud be hollerin' away at you at the top of their lungs that all the princes and awristycrats of Germany,

Italy, Denmark, Spain, England, Russia, Morocco, Holland, Egypt, Portugal, China, and Indochina have saw her and then went back to see her again, but Gentlemen, we ain't nuthin' like those charleytans and fairground ballyhooers who need to talk their merchandise up, and we run no risk in boastin' that in the case of our Zusabelle it's the meat, not the sauce, that draws the crowd.

GILES: We'll own up truthfully, Gentlemen, this incomparable Zirsabelle, afore comin' to France, has in actual fact bin in Ass-syria, Sweden, and even Bavaria, but there, as well as here, she guv only special performances on private stages and has never set foot in any public theatre, no, Gentlemen, and no one, either dead or alive kin boast of havin' ever saw her do it there, either in Paris or in the provinces, or in foreign parts, on this side of the ocean or across the seas.

THE PLAY

ISABELLE: (*Alone.*) I heartily wish that my pater dear's got his bizzness in as good shape as he'd like to make us believe; but in any case, it must be givin' him a bad case of the jitters to have obliged him to leave the house so early this morning with our valet Giles.

The good people, evidentally believin' I wuz sound asleep, haven't locked me up as usual. You see, they've fergot or they never knew that at my age a girl always has:

(*She sings the following verse.*)

A bee in her bonnet, an' love in her heart.

La puce à l'oreille .... l'amour .. z'au cœur

Dear me! On that subject, my late mudder dear always said, and with good reason, that a girl, afore bein' provided fer by marriage, wuz exposed to swallowin' many a bitter pill. Pore Zusabelle! Seems to me luv offers you no bedda roses. 'Smatter of fact, I dunno wot luv still has in store fer me, but that blastid infunt Kewpid's bin knockin' at my door and he duz it so pursistently in favor of the hansum Liander, our neighbor, that after all wuz sed 'n' done I cudn't keep him from gettin' in.

No, I don't understand myself, 'cos now here I am seventeen years old and after havin' saw myself catched four times by those nasty boys, how kin I at this time of day expose myself agin to the risk of a fifth adventure? Oh, why plunge into the affliction of a doubtful and uncertain sorrow? Lez resist as long as we kin, that's all very well! But once we're obliged to yield to force, lez do it with good grace; yes, and I think it's this latter course I gotta follow. When you come right down to it, wot do I have to reproach myself with? On the one hand, that dear Liander's bin bearin' down awful hard on my virtue for the past few days, and on the other hand, Mister Cassander, may father—whose soul may God receive if he jess happened to kick off suddenly—'s bin keepin' me and still's keepin' me under the constraint of such restrictive restrictions, especially since the death of my mudder dear, that he doesn't want so much as to even let into our house any male thing so I'd be reduced to never seein' one if, soon as him an' Giles is asleep, I hadn't made sure to git hold of the keys and come here every night to have a li'l bit of a confab with my dear Liander.

But despite the pleasure we git out of doin' it together, I feel it's takin' its toll on my peas and quiet and my strength of character'll finally give way in such an exhaustin' situation; a girl's not made of iron. So I've made up my mind for once that I'm gonna deliver myself from the slavery of such a captivity, and I wanna confer with my dearest belover about it. But here he is most oppertunely, and the old saying's right: talk of the devil and he is sure to appear.

(Enter Leander and his valet Harlequin.)

HARLEQUIN: Fer cryin' out loud, Sir! These young girls're sure some early risers once luv starts runnin' through their heads! It's barely seven o'clock and look, here's Mamselle Zusabelle already up an' rarin' to go, even though 'cording to the customs of the bourgeoisie she usually don't git up till eleven.

LEANDER: Leave us alone together and keep watch in the meanwhile so's we won't be sipprized.

HARLEQUIN: Oh, leave it to me; you know, Sir, it's not the first time Harleyquin's had the honor of plyin' the trade of coat-holder. *(Exit Harlequin.)*

LEANDER: My total beauty, I bin informed by my valet Harleyquin that your old oaf of a father's gone to Paris accompanied by Giles, and since my tender feelings of luv've made it an absolute law for me to seize each and every occasion to be with you, I'm takin' advantage of this favorable absence with the satisfaction of the greatest pleasure to spend this brief moment tellin' you about the bright flame of the fire of my burning ardor.

ISABELLE: Oh, dearest belover! I dunno where you come up with all the things you tell me, but you got ways of expressin' yourself that're more expressive than anybuddy else's expressions.

LEANDER: My divine creature, that's because your eyes're not made like those of the other girls, and accordin' to the military art I studied fer so long as a militia man, we deploy the artillery according to the terrain.

ISABELLE: Oh, how gallant!

LEANDER: Why, by golly! As the saying goes, honeyed words to suit the hear-
er, and it'd be preposterous to make the same preparations for the siege of
Port Mahon as to squash a riot in the local clink; speakin' of the clink, do
you realize I'd near as soon see myself engulfed in the depths of the abyss of
the most dreadful Black Hole than to live in the constraint in which yer
fathead of a father keeps you confined in.

ISABELLE: S'only too truly true to say that the fate of my destiny is much to
be bemoaned, but, where the goat is tethered, dearest belover, there it must
browse. So wot kin we do?

LEANDER: You ask wot kin we do? Wot everyone else duz in such cases and
wot I've already urged you to do many times. By golly, Mamselle, since
Mister Cassander doesn't wanna assent to the nuptials of our marriage, let
yourself be abduckted.

ISABELLE: Let myself be abduckted! Oh, dearest belover, I know you bin
tryin' to screw my courage to the sticking point, but lissen, it'd ill become
me to mince matters with you; and so I'll candidly admit it's not so much
bein' abduckted that frightens me as the manner of bein' abduckted.
Shudn't a well brung-up girl like me, who without overmuch prequivera-
tion is justly considered the most virtuous female in the vissinity of Montfaucon, where we wuz both native born, behave herself better'n anybuddy
else?

LEANDER: I agree, my luvable Zusabelle, but our marriage'll repair any
breach that mighta bin made . . .

ISABELLE: Oh, honest to gosh, haven't you knocked the wind outta my sails
and if marriage ain't a fine thing for repairin' the damage done to girls'
reputations! Once agin, dear Liander, I tell you: the blows I most fear at
the hands of the public are tongue-lashings; all the rest of it I find a laffin'
matter. Make your plans accordingly. Provided my pore reputation's kept
intact, I ask for nuthin' more, and if you discover how-to-do-it so's it won't
appear I consented to it, I hope thirty millions devils wring my neck if I
don't let myself be abduckted by you, ee-zee as ABC, at least twenty times
over.

LEANDER: Oh, my tasty li'l morsel, if we're only at loggerheads over the
manner of yer abducktion, in twenty-four hours you'll be mine hide and
hair, neck, crop, and heels. Depend on it, a li'l trifle like that's never fazed
me, and with the help of my tricky Harleyquin, I'd abduckt the favorite
wife of the Sultan of Monomotapa under the nose of his harem guard and
all his janissaries.

HARLEQUIN: (*Dashing in out of breath.*) Watch out fer dumb oxes. The old bozo
is at the end of the street, and Giles is comin' after him, Mamselle, loaded
down like a pack mule.

ISABELLE: (*With a tender expression.*) Leave me, dearest belover.

LEANDER: (*Kissing her hand.*) Oh, charming Zusabelle, when will you stop
assailin' me with such cruel discourse?

(*Exit Isabelle into the house.*)

HARLEQUIN: By profession I'm scarcely the type to git mixed up in other people's bizzness, unless I think I kin profit from it, be that said without offense to you, my dear master. Still, I'd be mighty curious to find out wot that numskull of a Giles is lugging around with such difficulty and which seems to make that old dodo Cassander so full of zip; but here they are. Lez hide and lissen. Mebbe sumpin' we'll overhear 'em say will put us wise.

(*Leander and Harlequin hide; enter Cassander and Giles, the latter loaded with a sack that seems to be very heavy.*)

CASSANDER: (*Stopping suddenly in his tracks.*) Giles?

GILES: Sir!

CASSANDER: Put that sack down. You look as if you wuz about to fold.

GILES: Foal? How am I sipposed to foal? Jess who do you take me fer? Do I look like a brood mare, or other such like beasts, Mister Cassander?

CASSANDER: O' course not! I only meant to tell you to set down that sack, so I kin chat with you here, afore goin' back into the house, without anybuddy eavesdroppin' on us.

GILES: (*Putting the sack on the ground.*) I don't at all go in fer that chatting, 'cos your bitch of a sack is so hefty that I got a powerful need to have a drink.

GILES: Alright, alright, that won't be long in comin' and I'll be short.

GILES: Oh, that won't be difficult for you, Sir, but so much the better, that's wot I like, and I don't at all agree with the late Madam Cassander who never stopped needlin' you about it.

CASSANDER: Oh, my poor Giles, lez leave the dead in peas.

GILES: Oh, Father Cassander, don't be scart, I ain't gonna respirate her behind so's to make her come back. Giles loves you too much for that.

CASSANDER: I'm not unawares of your devotion to me, so I'm gonna give you . . .

GILES: (*Holding out his hand.*) Oh, Sir . . .

CASSANDER: (*Finishing his sentences.*) A proof of my trust in you.

GILES: Too bad you wuzn't a girl, Sir!

CASSANDER: Why d'ya say that?

GILES: 'Cos then it wudn't 'a' cost you much of an outlay to make everybuddy's mouth water. But lez git back to brass tacks.

CASSANDER: This sack you find so heavy is actually sipposed to be that heavy, since besides a few ole togs, it contains twenty thousand crowns that b'long to me.

GILES: Twenty thousand crowns, Mister Cassander! Whodda thought it! But, without wantin' to be undooly curious, did ya rob a stagecoach? . . .

CASSANDER: Those twenty thousand crowns are the inheritance from my late cousin, Mister DePukkers, the night-soil man, whose sole heir I am.

GILES: Well, I'll be darned! I never wudda believed it paid off so big to stick one's nose in that there line of work!

CASSANDER: Now since idle money doesn't yield anything . . .

GILES: Meanin' no disrespeck, Father Cassander, it's clear you're in yer second dotage due to yer advanced age. Wotcha mean: idle money? Did ya ever see a crown loafin' round yawnin'?

CASSANDER: Are your brains mummified, my pore Giles! By idle money, we mean, as I wuz jess tellin' you, funds that don't yield anything. Now, so's not to fall into that error, I'm about to leave for Coulommiers with a confectioner from the rue des Lombards who's forced to sell his country house because of the sorry state of his bizzness.

GILES: Doggone it, Father Cassander, you must be pullin' my leg, tryin' to make me believe that in a town like Paris where all the talk is of taste and feeling, a maker of sweets goes bankrupt while a night-soil man gits rich. Oh, that's shocking to good sense and considerin' the hull thing carefully . . .

CASSANDER: Despite your inopportune and untimely reflections, it is none the less true. Now, during my trip, I leave you in charge of this precious treasure and of my dotter Zusabelle, advisin' you in particular not to let her talk to that big lummox of a Leander, who, notwithstanding my forbiddance, never stops perpetually prowlin' round our house.

GILES: You're right, Sir, once bit, twice shy. And besides, I sispeck the customer in question shares yer taste and in the way of girls especially likes funds that yield something. But lemme handle it, Sir, Giles is nobuddy's fool, Father Cassander; there's no outsmartin' him, and you kin hit the road whenever you feel like it.

CASSANDER: Coulommiers is but a few hours distant; the trip won't be long.

GILES: Oh, you cud be gone forever and a day, I wudn't care; I'll answer for all yer funds, and if, as they say, girls are like saltpeter, yours, Sir, runs the risk of farting sumpin' awful during your absence, 'cos I'll take care to keep her bottled up tight and this key won't leave my buttonhole.

CASSANDER: That's usin' the ole noggin, my dear Giles.

(*They carry the sack off together and go into the house.*)

HARLEQUIN: By golly, my dear master, that'd be a swell prize to git: twenty thousand crowns and a pretty girl who loves you.

LEANDER: 'Strue, Mamselle Zusabelle loves me and I cudn't have any doubts after the unequivocal proofs I git every day, and especially since the permission she's jess finally given me to abduckt her, but how to git round that animule Giles? You heard how Mister Cassander's forbadden him to let me talk to his dotter.

HARLEQUIN: Oh, 'slotsa things in this world that at first glance look confounded difficult to git into, and which on closer inspection prove the exack opposite. I'm not one to git easily discouraged, and this trip of Mister Cassander's gives me hope of findin', on mature reflection, a way of stealin' both the dotter and the twenty thousand crowns.

LEANDER: Oh, as fer the money, that's not wot tempts me, and although my late father—bless his simple soul—wuz only a dealer in rabbit skins, wot I got here in front is enuff to make Zusabelle happy and me as well.

HARLEQUIN: Oh, wot you got in front is all very well and good, but twenty thousand crowns added to it won't mar the household harmony, I shudn't think. Such outta-place disinterestedment gits me down, and to hear you talk, li'l children'd take you for one of them nasty ogres who relished only fresh meat. But . . . (*He rubs his forehead like someone thinking hard, then starts to laugh.*)

LEANDER: Wot's makin' you laff so hard?

HARLEQUIN: (*Still laughing.*) Lez git outta here fast, my dear master; the thought of you as an ogre's jess guv me another idea which, odd as it may seem, cud be a big success for us.

(*Exit Leander and Harlequin. Enter Cassander, Isabelle, and Giles.*)

CASSANDER: Once more, my dotter, I forbid you to speak to Leander. That man doesn't suit me any which way and I got my reasons for not likin' those girl-oglers.

ISABELLE: But whazza harm in that? A king may look at a cat, pater dear.

CASSANDER: Oh, he looks at wot he looks at and I forbid wot I forbid an' expeck to be obeyed. I tell you agin, Mamselle, I don't like skirt-chasers who from morning till midnight lie in wait for a girl like the fox by the henhouse door and never stop beatin' about the bush with her.

ISABELLE: Oh, I don't like 'em either, I assure you, but, thank heaven, Liander don't act that way towards me, and if you knew as I do, pater dear, the erectitude of his intentions . . .

CASSANDER: Oh, doggone it, no erectitude's gonna hold up your doin' wot I say, and I absotively order you to stay clear of him.

ISABELLE: Oh, pater dear, I'll never have the heart to do it.

CASSANDER: We'll see about that . . . Giles!

GILES: Sir!

CASSANDER: Remember, you'll have to answer for her behavior.

GILES: It's a ticklish ass-signment, but this key will answer for her behavior better'n I kin.

(*Exit Cassander.*)

GILES: Alright, Mamselle, git back into the house.

ISABELLE: Yes, perfidious wretch, I'm goin'. (*Aside.*) But if my dear belover keeps his promise it won't be for long, and this is wot's known as beatin' a tacktical retreat. (*Exit Isabelle.*)

GILES: Honest to gosh, whoever wuz right in sayin' that Fortune is mighty fickle wuzn't wrong; but then Fortune's a shemale and it's like they say, the weakest goes to the wall jess as sure as it never rains but it pours. Go ahead, ask me if that ole loon of a Cassander, crafty horse-flayer from Montfaucon and already filthy rich, needed to be included in the will of Father DePukkers, while as fer poor Giles, I cud see all the privy-cleaners and horse-skinners in Paris turn up their toes and never even inherit so much as a lousy barrel of shit or the skin offa dead dog.

(*Enter Leander and Harlequin in disguise.*)

HARLEQUIN: (*Carrying a pair of boots over his shoulders.*) Here's our man.

LEANDER: No, my dear Harleyquin, Giles cudn't possibly recognize us now, concealed as we are in the disguise of such a metamorphosis.

HARLEQUIN: Oh, by golly, I defy him to; I kin scarcely recognize myself.

GILES: Who are them funny birds after?

HARLEQUIN: If you back me up the way you shud, I give you my word: before long I'll make you master of both the key and the keyhole.

GILES: Now those are two perty mugs I can't place at all.

HARLEQUIN: He's lissenin' to us; lez broach the subjeck without seemin' to see him. (*In a loud voice to Leander.*) Yes, m'lord, you did the right thing, jess the right thing, exackly the right thing to turn down the one hundred thousand crowns that the Great Mogul offered you last night for that pair of boots.

GILES: Turn down one hundred thousand crowns for a pair of boots!

HARLEQUIN: (*Kissing the boots.*) Oh, dear boots, boots of my soul, if I wuz the owner of a similar treasure, I wudn't swop it for the whole Kingdom of Mesopotamia!

LEANDER: If I wuz right in rejectin' his offer, I acted with the discretion of a still greater circumspection in utilizin' the magical powers possessed by these divine boots to escape with all due haste from the realm of that wicked emperor who spoke of nuthin' less—as you well know—than of havin' me impaled right on the spot like a roasting turkey.

HARLEQUIN: Yes, indeed, that's jess wot wuz about to happen, and I wudn't 'a' got outta it any better. You see, it must be that those wicked folks don't much like Christianity! It wudn't be so bad if, in deprivin' you of yer boots, they'd 'a' made it up to you by givin' you the position of a Pasha of three tails, say, or of a white eunuch; I hear that's quite respectable and very lucrative but . . . wot's wrong, m'lord? You seem to be in a quandry of several dilemmas.

LEANDER: (*Rummaging through his pockets.*) Yes . . . There's a letter I agreed to deliver this evening to a banker in Paris and I fergot it this morning in Rome on the mantelpiece of Signor Scampini, who asked me to do him this favor.

GILES: He fergot it this morning in Rome! Ha! Ha! Ha! Ha! If that man ain't crazy, I do believe he's had more'n a few.

LEANDER: Gimme my boots so I kin go git that letter this very minute, and you stay here 'n' wait for me.

HARLEQUIN: You won't be long then, m'lord?

LEANDER: No, I'll jess step down there and back; it's no more than a few dozen brisk strides. (*Exit Leander.*)

HARLEQUIN: (*He pulls out a small grater and a plug of tobacco and says:*) If it'd bin me who fergot that letter, Idda bin an idiot, a rascal, a blockhead, a scatterbrain, a dolt, and all the rest, but since my master made the mistake, it's jess a tiny li'l peckerdillo not even worth mentionin'. (*He grates tobacco, as he sings the following song:*)

We'd be soulless bodies, dear tabaccy, without you nearby;
With you or the ladies, only a fool of boredom would die!

(*Harlequin does different lazzi, as he puts tobacco in his hand.*)

GILES: That man seems to be in high spirits and I'd like to strike up a conversation with him so's to worm a li'l sumpin' out of him.

HARLEQUIN: (*Offering him some tobacco.*) D'ya take snuff, Sir?

GILES: No, Sir, I don't take it, but sometimes I use it, if it's good.

HARLEQUIN: Oh, that bein' the case, you can try mine in total confidence, the Emperor of China never snorts any other kind, and I got this from his Royal Cotton-Bearer, who made me a present of two pounds of it last Monday in Peking.

GILES: In Peking! But, Sir, from what I bin told, I got the impression that it's a long way from here to Peking.

HARLEQUIN: Oh, no! It might be some five or six thousand leagues, at the very most.

GILES: Holy Moses! Izzat wot you call nuthin'?

HARLEQUIN: I'm not sayin' it's not a rather long journey for you and for others like you, but for my master and me, it's the merest trifle.

GILES: Well, I'll be! But, Sir, have you got some devil who gives you rides?

HARLEQUIN: Shame on you! Do you think the devil is a tote boy? I'll have you know we never travel anywhere 'cept on foot, and that's wot makes us go so fast.

GILES: Then did'ya git despleened? I hear that makes horses run faster.

HARLEQUIN: That's not it at all. As you don't appear to've had much education, it's not likely you've read or heard tell about how once upon a time there wuz a woodcutter and his wife who had seven boys; the last one havin' come into the world no bigger'n this (*he sticks up his thumb*) wuz called Tom . . .

GILES: . . . Thumb!

HARLEQUIN: That's right!

GILES: Sure, I know that story backwoods and forwoods, they used to rock me to sleep in my cradle with that one.

HARLEQUIN: Well, then, Tom Thumb, since Tom's the Thumb, knew how to thump so well that by . . . thumpin' away, Tom Thumb . . . thumped out other li'l Tom Thumbs who in turn thumped out others . . . from where there issued still others until, passed on from Tom Thumbs to Tom Thumbs, the famuss pair of seven-league boots have come down to my master, who is the last of the race of Thumbs.

GILES: Izzat possible?

HARLEQUIN: 'Sno less true than that you're a very brainy fellow.

GILES: (*Making a very deep bow and striking a pose.*) Oh, Sir!

HARLEQUIN: Well, those boots have another magical power not mentioned in the story: even though he doesn't have 'em on, the valet of the person wearin' the boots covers as much ground as his master does, when they travel together of course. So I bin round the world at least seven or eight hundred times since I joined my present master four years ago and left my hometown, Nogent-sur-Seine.

GILES: Wot! Are you from Nogent-sur-Seine?

HARLEQUIN: I sure am! Whazzo eggstrawdinary about that? Doesn't everyone have to be from somewhere?

GILES: Yes, that's true enuff, but by golly! I never wudda guessed it from the color of your face.

HARLEQUIN: I wuz as white as you when I left Nogent, and I turned this color as the result of a bad sunburn, but now I'm waitin' for the dew of May to clear it up.

GILES: Whadaya know! But tell me, dark and hansum, you musta knew Giles Bambino.

HARLEQUIN: That's some question, since I'm his neffew!

GILES: His neffew! So then you're Mother Bridoie's son?

HARLEQUIN: You bet I am, and that's why I'm called Bridoison.

GILES: (*Throwing his arms around his neck.*) Oh, by George, I'm so glad to see you, cousin!

HARLEQUIN: Whadaya mean, cousin?

GILES: Yes, by gosh, we're cousins, like it or not, since Giles Bambino is my father . . .

HARLEQUIN: (*Weeping.*) Oh, dear cousin, say he wuz your father, 'cos the pore man wuz buried a week ago and the day before yestidday I left your mother at death's door.

GILES: (*Weeping.*) My father dead and my mother at death's door, boo-hoo, boo-hoo, boo-hoo! That breaks my heart way down to the deepest depths of my guts, my dear cousin.

HARLEQUIN: It's true, cousin, that's mighty distressful, but the worse of all as I sees it is your absence from home, which kin be took advantage of by your cousin . . . you know the one . . . wot's his name?

GILES: Who do you mean? Cousin Riffart?

HARLEQUIN: Yes, cousin Riffart and his gawky stringbean of a wife, who's not worth . . .

GILES: But he's not married cousin; you mean his sister, long and lanky Michelle, don't ya?

HARLEQUIN: Oh, yes, that's right, long and lanky Michelle! If those two ain't the nastiest offshoots the devil ever brung forth! And you wudn't be the first they've fleeced of inheritances. Take it from me, I know it from bitter experience, and if it hadn't bin for them, worse luck, I wudn't be reduced to bein' in service the way I am.

GILES: But look here, cousin, wot's the cure for it?

HARLEQUIN: (*Reflecting.*) Honest to gosh, the best cure'd be your presence, and if I wuz you, I'd leave immejitly; a watchful eye keeps virtue strict, and you still might git there in time to have the pleasure of seein' yer por mother give up the ghost.

GILES: It's true that'ld be a great comfort to me, but I'm obliged to wait fer the return of my master, Mister Cassander, who left me to guard Mamselle Zusabelle, his dotter, and this house where with good reason I keep her locked up on his orders.

HARLEQUIN: And will his trip last long?

GILES: No, he shud be comin' back day after tomorrow at the very latest.

HARLEQUIN: Although that's not so very long from now, your pore mother cud quite easily cash in her chips in the meantime, if she hasn't done so already . . . But I got an excellent idea: if, considerin' how we're cousins, my master wud be willin' to lend you his boots, you cud take a flying leap back home this evening, once Isabelle's in bed, and as it only takes three strides and a li'l sumpin' more to go twenty-two leagues, yud have time to see wot's goin' on down there for yerself and git back before your mistress wakes up.

GILES: By golly, you got a head on your shoulders, cousin, but do you think your master'd be willin' to do me that favor?

HARLEQUIN: I'm not promisin' anything yet, even though he hardly ever turns me down, but we'll soon find out which way the wind blows, 'cos here he is.

(*Enter Leander.*)

GILES: Gosh almighty! That's some traveler! If everybody had boots like that, it wudn't pay to be postmaster general.

HARLEQUIN: Well, Sir, wot about that letter?

LEANDER: (*Handing the letter to Harlequin.*) Here it is, and all you have to do is deliver it this evening to the address written on the envelope. But who is this man?

HARLEQUIN: Sir, this is my first cousin, the son of that pore deceased Giles Bambino, my uncle, whose widder—as you well know—we left on her deathbed. I have a li'l favor to ask you on his behalf and I beg you not to turn me down.

LEANDER: Jess wot is it a question of being in reference to?

HARLEQUIN: As his presence is required back home and as we'll be stayin' here for two days, during which time yer boots won't be of any use to you, the question, Sir, is whether yud lend them to him until tomorrow.

LEANDER: Lend my boots! But you can't be serious! Are boots like these sumpin' one lends? And then, besides, wud he know how to make usage of them?

HARLEQUIN: On the score of trustworthiness, you're not runnin' any risk, Sir; in my fambly there's never bin anything but the uprightest folks, you know that, and with regard to the manner of usin' these boots, it won't take more'n a moment to put wise somebuddy with as sound instincts as cousin Giles.

GILES: Oh, you're so kind-hearted, cousin.

LEANDER: Then you'll be responsible for him?

HARLEQUIN: As I wud for myself.

GILES: (*Throwing himself at Leander's feet.*) And you can trust me, Lord of Tom Thumbery, I'll answer fer yer boots body an' soul.

LEANDER: Alright, pull my boots off, and we'll see if the brilliance of his perspicacity is as vast as you say it is.

HARLEQUIN: (*Takes Leander's boots off and puts them on Giles with many a lazzi.*) Alright, shake a leg, cousin!

GILES: (*Falls down.*) Oops, oops! It's lucky I landed on my nose.

HARLEQUIN: That's right, it kept you from smashing your cheek-bones and that's all there is to it. Quick now, lift the other leg.

GILES: (*Falls down again.*) Oops, oops, oops! Boy, this apprenticeship strikes me as a rough sort of roughment!

HARLEQUIN: Oh, o' course, cousin, you never git anything in this world without a certain immount of pain, and anyhoo, there's always sumpin' to be thankful fer, 'cos now you're in jess the right position to take your first lesson.

GILES: (*Sitting up*) What a bitch of a ceremony!

LEANDER: (*While Harlequin fastens Giles's two spurs together with a piece of string, Leander takes a rope out of his pocket with which he ties Giles's arms, saying:*) Look, here's the famuss cord spun outta her own hair by the fairy Arpentina, who preserves from danger all travelers who've had the good fortune once in their lives to be tied up by her.

(*Leander takes the key from Giles without his noticing and goes into Isabelle's house while Harlequin distracts Giles.*)

HARLEQUIN: (*With a mysterious air, takes a burnt cork and draws large handle-bar mustaches on Giles and a half-mask that covers his chin, saying:*) That's the final operation, now you can go to hell and back without the slightest fear, but as you seem a bit tired, cousin, I'm gonna join my master who went to git a bottle of Father Cassander's wine so's to give you a drink.

GILES: Wot are you talkin' about, cousin?

HARLEQUIN: See ya round. (*Exit Harlequin.*)

GILES: (*Alone, seeing Harlequin go into Cassander's house and noticing that he no longer has his key, makes futile efforts to get free and says:*) Oh, wretch, wot have I done? My pore key! That dog of a scoundrelly cousin! Stop thief! Call the guard! Police! Fire!

ISABELLE: (*In the house, screams at the same time.*) Save me, Giles! Help! Murder! (*Isabelle appears, led by one hand by Leander, and by the other by Harlequin who is carrying the sack; she says to Giles:*) Oh, you rascal Giles! To let me be abduckted like this before your very eyes! Izzat wot you promised my dear pater? Rest assured that if I'm ever able to send him news of my precious whereabouts, I won't fergit to tell him to have you hanged.

LEANDER: All your cries are in vain, Mamselle, and you're comin' with us.

HARLEQUIN: So long, cousin, bon voyage. If you always burn up the roadways at that rate, the soles of yer boots'll last you a lifetime.

(*Exit Leander, Isabelle, and Harlequin.*)

GILES: (*Alone.*) Oh, bandits! Oh, double-crossers! Sons of Cain! But wot will my dear master say when he sees his money and his dotter abduckted? Won't he go and think I wuz mixed up in it all?

(*Enter Cassander.*)

CASSANDER: My trip's bin put off till tomorrow, and I'm not too irked 'cos after all it'll give me time to wind up some bizzness.

GILES: (Not seeing Cassander.) Oh, poor Father Cassander, wot's gonna become of you?

CASSANDER: Wot's this I see? Giles tied up? And wot do these boots mean?

GILES: (Turning around.) Oh, whoever you are, take pity on me!

CASSANDER: (Terrified, drawing back.) Oh, cud it be some gobblelin that's put on Giles's clothes to frighten me? Yes, 'sno doubt about it, it's my late missis who's playin' this here trick on me!

GILES: Oh, no, Sir, it's me, I swear it!

CASSANDER: And jess who got you all rigged up like that?

GILES: Woe is me! How kin I explain it to you? That good-fer-nuthin' of a cousin Bridoison, who's the biggest rascal, Sir, the world's ever saw . . . my pore father buried eight days ago . . . my mother at death's door . . . Rome . . . the great Mogul . . . Peking . . . the Emperor of China's Royal Cotton-Bearer . . . Nogent-sur-Seine . . . the Pasha of three tails . . . Isabelle . . . then Tom Thumb . . . and . . . how do I know wot all?

CASSANDER: Wot kind of infernal gibberish izzat you're talkin'? He musta went crazy, and 'sno wonder they decided to tie him up.

GILES: Oh, no, Sir, I'm not crazy; wot I bin tellin' you's only too truly true, and to cut a long story short, Isabelle's bin abduckted.

CASSANDER: Wot! My dotter abduckted! And you let sumpin' like that happen?

GILES: Oh, I wudda let a lot more happen in the state I wuz in, and if yud bin in my place, you wudn't 'a' bin able to stop them from carryin' off yer dotter or the sack either.

CASSANDER: (Grabbing him by the collar.) Wot, you lout! My sack's bin ab-duckted too? . . . Oh, wretch, you'll be hanged, and had you ten thousand lives, I'd rip 'em all outta yer body one by one!

(Enter Leander and Isabelle.)

LEANDER: (In his normal clothes, holding Isabelle by the hand.) The constellation of the happy star of my lucky planet havin' caused me to come runnin' in answer to the cries of Mamselle, whom four brigands were attemptin' to force bodily into a wagon at the foot of Montfaucon, my customary valor enabled me efficaciously to extricate her from their clutches, and I come, Sir, with the greatest of pleasure to give her back into your hands.

CASSANDER: And my sack, Sir, my sack?

LEANDER: My valet, Harleyquin, 's right behind us, and he's bringin' it back to you.

(Enter Harlequin carrying the sack.)

HARLEQUIN: I dunno wot's in there, but it's confounded heavy in its pon-
derosity.

CASSANDER: (*To Leander, who helps Harlequin set down the sack.*) Oh, Sir, how
kin I ever repay you for such a service?

LEANDER: The object of my affection havin' long bin known to you, Sir,
you've only to scratch me where it itches by accordin' me the luvable hand
of the charming Zusabelle.

CASSANDER: It'd be unjust of me to deny you a part of wot I'd no longer have
without yer help; so I give you Zusabelle with all my heart, and I keep the
sack.

HARLEQUIN: Half a loaf is better'n no bread!

ISABELLE: Many thanks, pater dear. On account of I'm gittin' married, I pardon Giles, although I'd bin countin' on havin' the pleasure of seein' him
hanged.

CASSANDER: That's wot I'd bin hopin' for too, but I pardon him also, my
dotter.

HARLEQUIN: Things bein' the way they is, I'm gonna give him the key of the
street to make up for the key he had took away from him.

GILES: (*Making a leap.*) I got outta this a lot better'n I thunk I wud, and
'smatter of fact I wuz scart stiff my trip wud end up leavin' me hangin' in
mid-air.

END

Courtesy: KaiDib Films International, Glendale, California

THEATRE IN ŁAŃCUT (ca. 1784)

Photo: Zbigniew Raplewski;

FOUR PARADES

Jan Potocki

Franciszek Myszkowski

A PARADE by Jan Potocki (Dramatic Theatre, Warsaw, 1958)

Franciszek Myszkowski

A PARADE by Jan Potocki (Dramatic Theatre, Warsaw, 1958)

GILES IN LOVE

A Parade in One Act and in Prose

CHARACTERS:

Zerzabelle, discretely dressed in a morning negligée
Giles, coquettishly got up

The action takes place in a village, in front of Zerzabelle's house.

GILES: (*Alone.*) There's no denying I'm a most unhappy Giles. Other Gileses are always laughing and joking. But I'm so sad. Mister Leander, now he's the one who should be in love with Mamzelle Zerzabelle. And yet I'm the one who actually is. The whole trouble is that this here Mamzelle Zerzabelle was born a lady just to make my life miserable. Oh, if she was only an ordinary she-Giles like me, I'd have told her . . . Oh, no, I'd never have dared tell her that, because she'd have answered me, "Giles!" And I'd never have been able to stand that tone of voice. I didn't have any idea there was so much to be miserable about in this world. If I'd known, I'd never have come here in the first place. Because getting out is no easy matter. Sure, I know you can run a sword through your body, but how's that help, if no one ever bothered to teach me to bear arms? Sure, I know you can throw yourself in the river, and I'd certainly drown myself if I knew how to swim. Because as far as poisons go, I don't even know what anecdotes to take with them. They tell me it's all due to my stars, but I looked up at the sky all night long and I couldn't see a single thing. Now here's where Mamzelle Zerzabelle's pretty little feet go in and out of the house. Although those little feet are not so very big, I love them much, much more than if they were the feet of any majesty the king. Shush! I hear Mamzelle Zerzabelle's feet coming down the stairs of the house. Giles, you'd better hide.

(*Exit Giles and enter Zerzabelle.*)

ZERZABELLE: (*Alone.*) Giles was just here. He can't be far away. Where could he have gone? I have so much trouble getting to meet him, and then when I do succeed, the merest trifle scares him away and he gives me the slip. I am foolish to love a Giles, but it's stronger than I am. They tell me I have brains enough for four, then maybe I'll have enough for two. For some time now, he's been daydreaming and talking to himself—he's in love, I'm sure of it. But is he in love with me? I haven't been able to find out yet for sure. He can't be far from here; I'm going to call him on the pretext of sending him on some errand or other. Giles! Giles!

(*Re-enter Giles.*)

GILES: Here I am, Mamzelle.
ZERZABELLE: Giles, I wanted to ask you to go . . .
GILES: I'm off, Mamzelle.
ZERZABELLE: Wait, just where were you planning to go?
GILES: I don't know, Mamzelle, and I don't care either. Because when you send me somewhere, I go there immediately and don't even ask where.
ZERZABELLE: So you're in a great hurry to leave me.
GILES: I'm capable of it, if it's to serve you.
ZERZABELLE: My dear Giles!
GILES: (*Aside.*) Oh, I wasn't ready for that "My dear Giles." I almost gave my secret away asskidentally.
ZERZABELLE: Giles, have you ever been in love?
GILES: And why do you ask me that, Miss?
ZERZABELLE: Why? Just out of curiosity.
GILES: Out of curiosity! Isn't that just like a young lady! You're curious to know if a Giles can fall in love.
ZERZABELLE: I don't want to know if you can fall in love. I want to know if you are in love.
GILES: And suppose I was in love, Miss, would I come tell you I was?
ZERZABELLE: What does he mean by that? Giles! Is the one you love a young lady?
GILES: A young lady! A young lady! Do you think I have such a high opinion of myself?
ZERZABELLE: Oh, heavens! The one he loves is not a lady. Then it's not me. I'm so unhappy.

GILES: Oh! My god, my god! Mamzelle Zerzabelle is in a bad way and it's all my doing. Where can I hide? Where can I hide? (*He hides.*)

ZERZABELLE: Wouldn't you know it! He's gone off again somewhere. It's enough to make a person lose all patience. How can I be so witless that with all the means at my disposal I still cannot get my own way? But I won't be denied. Either I'll die in the process or I'll find out right now whether he loves me or someone else. Giles! Giles! Oh! How can you let me go on calling you for such a long time?

GILES: Oh! Mamzelle, it's so nice when you call me like that, who'd think of saying, "I'm coming"? You could keep on calling me all day long and I wouldn't . . .

ZERZABELLE: That'll do, that'll do. Stay right where you are. I have something to tell you, and no matter what happens, don't go off anywhere.

GILES: Oh! As for not going off anywhere, Mamzelle, well that won't be so very difficult. Because, you see, even if I went, I wouldn't go anywhere.

ZERZABELLE: Tell me something, Giles. Did you get up a long time ago?

GILES: Oh! As for getting up, Mamzelle, that's something that never did happen to me at all, since I didn't go to bed all night long.

ZERZABELLE: You didn't go to bed? What did you do then?

GILES: What did I do, Mamzelle? What I did was I didn't do anything at all. And that's all I did from the dawn of night to the dusk of daybreak. (*Aside.*) How about that! There was a neatly turned phrase. First time it ever happened to me.

ZERZABELLE: But, Giles, it seems to me that if I thought about one thing all night long, I'd mention it sometime during the day.

GILES: Oh, no! You won't catch me with that one, Mamzelle. Now, if I think to myself and you overhear my thoughts, well, it won't be my fault. But if I talked out loud, and you didn't want to hear what I was saying, well, then it would be my fault. And you see, Mamzelle, that secret of mine is my whole treasure. So it's only natural I'd want to guard something so precious.

ZERZABELLE: (*Aside.*) He's beginning to be quite touching. (*To Giles.*) Giles, you can entrust your secret to me. I'll guard it as if it were my own.

GILES: Oh, no! You won't catch me with that one, Mamzelle. I know the young ladies; they like a good laugh. They worm your secret out of you, and then once they've got an "I love you," they drop you cold and sneer right in your face. Look here, Mamzelle, I'm not so stupid I don't understand exactly what you mean to tell me when you say: "Giles, come here," and "Giles, go there," and "What are you thinking about when you're not thinking about anything," and "Why are you awake when you're not asleep?"

ZERZABELLE: The impudent boy! He understood my confession of love and hasn't responded to it.

GILES: So you see, Mamzelle, it's like in the saying that flowers often hide under the innocent serpent. And all the same it's . . .

ZERZABELLE: Yes, yes, that will do, that will do! You figured it out, I only wanted to have a little fun while I was waiting for Mister Leander, who's supposed to come today . . . But what's the matter with you?

GILES: (*Weeping and getting down on his knees.*) Oh, Mamzelle! You were only having your fun and waiting for Mister Leander. And what's even worse, it's all my fault that I displeased you and right now I'm even more unhappy than when I was so wretched this morning. But, Mamzelle, this won't last any longer than the time it takes for me to go down to the river and as soon as I get there, I'll put a rope around my neck, throw myself in the water, and hang until drowned.

ZERZABELLE: No, my dear Giles, don't drown yourself. I love you, you're the one I'm going to marry, and everything I said was only to arouse your jealousy.

GILES: Oh, my god! That wasn't necessary. I've got more than I can use; I could let you have some.

ZERZABELLE: Keep it to yourself, my dear Giles! Excess jealousy serves no useful purpose. And just now if I went out of my way to make you jealous, I did it only to discover your secret so that I could entrust the care of my happiness to you.

GILES: Oh, Mamzelle! All the happiness will be on my side.

ZERZABELLE: Let it be on both sides, since you never can be happy unless I am happy too.

END

CASSANDER'S TRIP TO THE INDIES

A Parade

CHARACTERS:

Cassander, Zerzabelle's Father
Zerzabelle, Cassander's Daughter
Leander, Young Man in Love with Zerzabelle
Giles, Cassander's Valet

The action takes place along the boulevards or on a street.

CASSANDER: (*Alone.*) Yes, the more I think about it, the more convinced I become of the absolute necessity of getting away from here through the expedient of no longer being present. Respectable people are always the most exposed to slander, and ever since I was hung in Iphigenia before the eyes of the astonished multitude, my commerce and my credit have suffered considerably. The best families avoid me everywhere, as soon as they run into me. When I pass by, little boys point the finger of scorn at me. In short, everything conspires to make my stay at Chaillot repugnant to me.

  So the best thing for me to do is to have my old mule saddled up and spur the steed on for the West East Indies, a country from which everyone comes back with his pockets lined with gold.

  But before setting out, I must put everything to rights in my house so that the strictest order will be ineffably maintained.

  In particular, I must give some thought to my daughter Zerzabelle. For almost thirty years now she's been in a highly marriageable state, and the preservation of her virtue burdens me with cares of near-fatal solicitude.

Giles! Giles!
Why doesn't that rascal come? Giles! Giles!

(He goes into the wings and leads in Giles, pulling him by the ear.)

CASSANDER: Well! Why don't you come when you're called?

GILES: But, Mister Cassander, I didn't hear anything.

CASSANDER: What! You didn't hear anything, you rascal! We'll soon see whether or not you heard anything. *(He shouts, "Giles! Giles!" And then he dashes into the wings to find out if his voice can be heard.)* He's right, by jove! You can't hear anything at all.

GILES: That's just what I was telling you. And you din't have to pull my ear so hard; I just don't like that sort of handshake.

CASSANDER: Come now, it's all right. I have something important to tell you. So lend me your ear, and pay attention.

GILES: Oh, no, Sir! You won't catch me with that one. I'm not willing to lend you my ears again. The use you put them to was much, much too nasty.

CASSANDER: You misunderstand me; I simply mean you must listen carefully to what I have to say.

GILES: Oh! No problem there, Sir, I'll listen all you like, provided you let me finish snoozing a little nap I started back in the house.

CASSANDER: Don't you get any ideas about sleeping, you scoundrel, or I'll wake you up in a way you won't find in the least bit pleasing.

GILES: Oh, no thanks, Sir! Don't go to any trouble. All right, I'm listening.

CASSANDER: Well, then, Giles! You should know that I am about to leave on a trip.

GILES: Oh! Well, bon voyage, Sir. *(He leaves.)*

CASSANDER: Where do you think you're going? I haven't yet told you where I'm going.

GILES: So whuzzat to me?

CASSANDER: But, Giles, you should know that I'm going to the Indies via Greece and Turkey.

GILES: Grease and turkey, well, all right! I don't much care about the grease, but if it's roast turkey, I'll come along with you.

CASSANDER: You're wide of the mark, my dear Giles. The Indies are a far-off country where people go to inherit fortunes.

GILES: Do you have any relatives there?

CASSANDER: No, all my relatives are in Chaillot. But I've already told you that people go to the Indies to inherit fortunes, and if you hit on a good year, you can well imagine . . . *(Cassander claps Giles on the shoulder.)*

GILES: Yes, I can well imagine; you're going to inherit a fortune in the form of a turkey, and I hope for my part, I'll get a leg or a wing.

CASSANDER: Yes, that's it exactly. This time you understood me perfectly.

But I also wanted to tell you that my absence will be a long one.

GILES: You absence will be a long one? How long? Full-length?

CASSANDER: I mean it'll be a long time before I return.

GILES: How about that! So much the better! There'll be fewer of us at table, and you know the old saying: "The fewer fools at table, the more to eat for everyone." And then, since there was enough to eat for three before, now there'll even be enough for me to eat, especially if I don't give any to Miss Zerzabelle.

CASSANDER: Be quiet and let me do the talking. It's precisely about my daughter that I want to have a word with you.

I know she is as virtuous as she is beautiful. But that's just an additional danger. And I have every reason to fear that, carried away by the ardor of a new passion, she'll throw her virtue to the winds and fall into the snares set for her by a certain Leander, who every evening prowls around our house. That's why, my dear Giles, I'd like us to consider ways of stopping this Leander from ever coming back or even showing his face here again.

GILES: Hey! Nothing simpler. All we have to do is give him one hundred blows with a big stick the first time he shows his face here.

CASSANDER: That's not a bad plan, but I think you should know that he always carries a long sword with him.

GILES: Dammit! I didn't know that! Then the only way is to give him the hundred blows with a big stick without him noticing it.

CASSANDER: That's right, but how are we going to do it?

GILES: You got me. It's up to you to figure it out.

CASSANDER: I've got a feeling that's going to prove too difficult. The simplest thing will be for you to station yourself in front of the door to our house and prevent him from coming in. But it's getting late. The Indies are a long way off. I must be going. Adieu, my dear Giles, do your duty. Don't expect me for supper. So eat up everything yourself and save what's left over for me. (*Exit Cassander.*)

GILES: (*Alone.*) Sure, you can betcha life I'll save you something! If I eat up everything, I certainly should be able to eat what's left over too. And what about in-between meals? Don't I do any eating then too?

Mister Cassander told me to stay here in front of the door, but he didn't tell me not to go to sleep here. And then, even if he'd told me a hundred times, how's my sleeping going to make any difference? And then, I'll always have time to wake up if Mister Leander gets the urge to prowl around the house. Let's go to bed! My god, how hard it is! If only they'd thought of putting a little straw under the paving stones, at least on the place where I have to lie down! That wouldn't have cost them much, and it would have shown a little consideration for me. (*He sings.*)

See pretty Lisa sleeping in a grove,

Her two arms here, another over there . . .

(*He falls asleep.*)

(*As he comes in, Leander falls on top of Giles. They both get up and exchange bows.*)

LEANDER: May I know, Sir, on whom I have just now had the honor of falling?

GILES: On me, Sir. And you, Sir, couldn't you tell me who has done me the honor of falling on top of me?

LEANDER: It was I myself, Sir. Leander is the name, at your service.

GILES: Izzat so? In that case, Sir, I humbly request you to look in the other direction, without paying any attention to what I'm doing.

LEANDER: And what's the reason for that, Sir?

GILES: Because I have instructions to give you one hundred blows with a big stick, without you noticing it.

LEANDER: Don't go to the trouble, Sir, because I am every bit as obliged to you as if you had actually given them to me.

GILES: Oh, no, Sir! It's no trouble! And especially when it's for a distinguished gentleman like you. Without taking into account that Mister Cassander, when he comes back from the Indies, will be very glad to see I've carried out the assignment he charged me with.

LEANDER: Oh! So Mister Cassander went to the Indies.

GILES: Yes, and he won't be back this evening. So whenever you like, we can begin.

LEANDER: It's not urgent. You say Mister Cassander has charged you to give me one hundred blows with a big stick.

GILES: That's right, Sir, with my very own hands! So as to prevent you from coming in to see Mademoiselle Zerzabelle, and that's the only reason why I went to sleep here.

LEANDER: What, you scoundrel! So your imbecile of a master, Cassander, wants to prevent me from coming in to see Miss Zerzabelle? But I really don't have any desire to.

GILES: But where are you going then?

LEANDER: I'm coming out from the Boulevards and your master has no right to stop me.

GILES: No, certainly not! But if you're coming out from the Boulevards through the door to our house, then you'll find yourself in our house.

LEANDER: Well, what of it? I won't have come in and your master only ordered you not to let me in. And then I'll tell you something else. I have here a one thousand pistole sack, in which at the moment there is only one gold crown worth three francs. This gold crown is for you, if you let me through here.

GILES: Sir, I'd like it better if you had a one gold crown sack, in which there were a thousand pistoles. But give it to me anyway and come in. I won't stop you.

(*Exit Leander.*)

GILES: Mister Cassander will be absolutely astounded when he sees that Mister Leander has been in his house without ever having come in. I have the impression they're up to something in there right now. But here's Mister Cassander himself. (*Enter Cassander.*)

CASSANDER: It has to be said that trips of long duration are subject to the most variable vicissitudes. I passed through Passy and Saint-Cloud; I came back to Asnière; everywhere I asked where the Indies were! No one could tell me. But here's Giles! Well, how about it, my friend? Did you do your duty? No one came in the house, did they?

GILES: No, Sir.

CASSANDER: Then Mister Leander didn't fall into the trap we set for him?

GILES: No, Sir, he only fell on top of me and dislocated my shoulder.

CASSANDER: How was that?

GILES: Like this! (*He falls on Cassander, knocks him over and falls down too.*)

CASSANDER: Oh, you confounded clumsy fool! So Mister Leander did come.

GILES: Yes, Sir.

CASSANDER: And did you give him the hundred blows with a big stick, as we agreed?

GILES: No, Sir.

CASSANDER: And why not?

GILES: Because he said it wasn't urgent and he was just as obliged to me as it was.

CASSANDER: In any case, he didn't come in the house.

GILES: No, Sir, he came out.

CASSANDER: He came out from where?

GILES: From the Boulevards.

CASSANDER: So you chased him away?

GILES: What do you mean! He's been in the house for over an hour.

CASSANDER: Oh, you wretch! Oh, you rogue!

(*Zerzabelle and Leander throw themselves at Mister Cassander's feet.*)

ZERZABELLE: Oh, my dear father! I throw myself at your feet and beg you to bring an end to this fatal widowhood to which my maiden state condemns me. I have chosen Leander for my husband.

CASSANDER: What? Without consulting me? No, I'll never consent to that.

ZERZABELLE: Oh, my father! Let yourself be swayed. At least on account of my condition . . .

CASSANDER: Your condition . . . Wretched girl! Since when?

ZERZABELLE: Since more than half an hour ago.

CASSANDER: Oh, ungrateful girl, is this the celibacy that I expected of you?

LEANDER: Sir, if you would deign to hear me, I should point out to you that the Leanders of all times have married the Zerzabelles and the Cassanders have always received a good drubbing. So if you refuse to give me the hand of your daughter, I shall be compelled to give you one hundred kicks in the stomach.

CASSANDER: Kicks in the stomach? Wait a moment. My entrails speak for you, my daughter. Still, Sir, I cannot believe that you would wish to affront me thus in my own presence.

LEANDER: You'll forgive me, Sir, but I'll do just what I said.

CASSANDER: Well, then! Let's not say another word about it. Your mutual tenderness touches me deeply. And nothing further will oppose the extreme happiness of your felicity.

ZERZABELLE: Oh, my father!

LEANDER: Oh, Sir!

END

CASSANDER, MAN OF LETTERS

A Parade in One Act and in Prose

CHARACTERS:

Cassander
Zerzabelle
Leander
Doctor

The action takes place in Cassander's house.

CASSANDER: Sit down, my daughter! I wish to have a private soliloquy with you about the son-in-law, whose father-in-law I have decided to be. Such being the case, lend an attentive discourse to the ears I am about to address to you.

ZERZABELLE: My dear father, the subject of your discourse interests me immensely, and if your choice agrees with mine, I shall obey you without the slightest aversion.

CASSANDER: I expected no less from your indocility. You know, my dear Zerzabelle, you are the only only child who has remained to me of the more than twenty twins brought into the world by Madam Cassander. She died, alas, and left you in my arms, a posthumous orphan without mother or father. From that very moment, I resolved to devote my entire life to the cares of your education. I became your Juliet, you were my Romeo, whom I took delight in adorning with talent, charm, and virtue. To be equal to the task, I decided to become a man of letters. I bought myself a position as beadle at the university and opened my house to the greatest wits from the mausoleum of innocents.

ZERZABELLE: But, my dear father, how could you become a man of letters, when you can't even read or write?

CASSANDER: You're wide of the mark there, my girl. Literature is not quite what you think it is. To be a man of letters it suffices to serve dinner on Sundays to those who do know how to read and write.

And so, my dear Zerzabelle, I have devised a project that should cover us both with glory. I am going to establish a competition, and whoever composes the most beautiful treatises on various subjects will become my son-in-law, and you, my dear Zerzabelle, will have the honor of being an academic prize.

ZERZABELLE: But father! What the devil does all that nonsense mean? If I do marry, it will be to become a wife and not some academic prize. And all those treatises won't have any effect on me, I can assure you!

CASSANDER: My daughter, you are adopting a very strange tone about all this. Would you have the effrontery to dispose of your heart, without first having asked for my hand?

ZERZABELLE: Yes, my father, I am in love and if you try to thwart my inclinations, I have resolved to hurl myself headlong into a convent.

CASSANDER: And may one know the name of the happy mortal whom you have chosen?

ZERZABELLE: My father, the one I love is no ordinary mortal, he is Mister Leander, and he's a corporal in the mercenary guard.

CASSANDER: What do I hear? The daughter of a man of letters to become the wife of a corporal! Oh, ungrateful girl! Have I then nourished you in the bosom of a viper only so you could become the shame of your family? But nothing of the sort will ever take place. I'm going to the Doctor's this very instant, and I insist you marry him this evening without any prize or competiton. Besides, he's certainly the one who would have won the prize for those treatises. Adieu, I'll be right back. (*Exit Cassander.*)

ZERZABELLE: (*Alone.*) He's gone, leaving me a prey to feelings of loneliness. If only Leander would appear now . . . But what do I see? It's the mailman from the corner post office bringing me an epistle. It's from Leander. He's sealed it with a wax seal. Most likely it contains secrets. But what does that matter! I simply must read it aloud.

"Dearest belover: Far from you, eternities seem but hours, and the minutes pass like instants. If I were by your side, absence would be the merest trifle. And that is why I shall not fail to come tonight while the iron's ripe and the early bird makes hay, or as the saying goes, a stitch in the nick of time. Having the honor of being your Leander."

Oh, my, here's a fine state of affairs! Mister Leander will come tonight while the iron's ripe and the early bird makes hay. And in the meantime I'll have become an academic prize for the Doctor. What should I do? What ruse should I devise? But what do I see? It's Leander himself. Oh, dearest belover!

(*Enter Leander.*)

LEANDER: Oh, my adored belover!

ZERZABELLE: Oh, dearest belover! I am losing you forever!

LEANDER: What's that you're saying?

ZERZABELLE: Yes, nothing is more certain. This very evening I am to become an academic prize.

LEANDER: What? But perhaps that won't prevent you from becoming my wife?

ZERZABELLE: There's not the slightest doubt about it. This evening the Doctor . . .

LEANDER: Oh, my! This evening the Doctor . . .

ZERZABELLE: Yes, this evening the Doctor is going to give me . . .

LEANDER: Oh, my! What is he going to give you?

ZERZABELLE: He's going to give me . . . I don't have the courage to finish . . .

LEANDER: He's going to give you . . .

ZERZABELLE: He's going to give me a treatise.

LEANDER: Oh, Zerzabelle! Don't be afraid! I won't leave you and before he can get hold of his treatise, I'll run my sword all the way through his body. Oh, arms, legs, head, stomach! Oh, vital organs!

(*While Leander paces up and down swearing, Cassander comes in with the Doctor. They all collide and fall on top of one another. As he gets up, Leander picks up the Doctor's cloak and puts it on. Everyone gets up and bows.*)

CASSANDER: I do hope that you didn't hurt yourself, Doctor.

DOCTOR: Quite on the contrary.

CASSANDER: But look, here's a gentleman who's done us the honor of falling down with us and yet whom I don't have the honor of knowing. He certainly must be one of the men of letters who have been drawn here, once they got wind of the competition I've established.

ZERZABELLE: Say yes.

LEANDER: Yes, Sir, as a matter of fact I am one of those men of . . . what do you call them?

CASSANDER: A man of letters.

LEANDER: Yes, a man of letters drawn here by the competition of wind that you're making.

DOCTOR: Now, in that case, Sir, you can see that, I am ready to carry on a dispute with you on whatever subject you like and in any language you may be pleased to choose. Do you prefer that we speak Hebrew, Chaldean, Syriac, Latin, or Greek?

LEANDER: Very well, Sir! Why don't you speak Greek?

DOCTOR: With the greatest of pleasure. Here is my theme:
   Menin aedie, thea, Peleiadee Achileos
   oulomene, e myri' Achaiois alge etheke.

LEANDER: Who did that Greek, Sir?

DOCTOR: Who did that Greek? Can you ask me? Oh! Who could have done it but Homer? Who but Homer has spoken the language of the Gods? Who but Homer . . .

LEANDER: Oh, run along with your beachcomber! Listen here, if you have your Greek done by beachcombers, I make up mine myself, and soon you'll be able to judge for yourself.
   Oh, tune your oboes, Procne and Philomele,
   To sing with joy of Cassander and Zerzabelle,
   Or rather sing of Zerzabelle and Cassander,
   So tune your oboes to a tone most tender.

ZERZABELLE: Oh, my god! That's so beautiful! That's so beautiful!

CASSANDER: Yes, it actually is very beautiful.

DOCTOR: It may be extremely beautiful, but Sir, you'll allow me to point out to you: it's not Greek.

LEANDER: What's that? It's not Greek? I tell you it is Greek.

ZERZABELLE: It certainly is Greek, it certainly is Greek.

CASSANDER: And it must be very good Greek indeed, since I understood it perfectly.

DOCTOR: But, Sir, I can prove to you . . .

LEANDER: But, see here, our would-be Doctor, you are very bold to dare maintain to Mister Cassander . . .
   Yes, Mister Cassander, one has to be very bold indeed to come offer a man like you Greek by a beachcomber and if I were you . . .

(*Meanwhile, Zerzabelle grabs the Doctor by the shoulders and drives him out, shouting at him: "Get out of here, get out of here!"*)

CASSANDER: Yes, Sir, you're right. And as for you, learned Doctor, I tell you that . . . But he's not here any more. Evidently he considered himself beaten.

ZERZABELLE: My dear father, how could he consider himself otherwise, since I, for my part, gave him more than twenty swift kicks.

CASSANDER: Izzat so? Then in that case, Sir, nothing can any longer obstruct the impediments that stood in the path of your felicity. I give you my daughter and I confer upon you after my death all the income that I receive from my investments.

LEANDER: Oh, Sir! I cannot accept . . .

CASSANDER: No, Sir, that is the way I want it to be.

END

CASSANDER SUPPORTS THE REVOLUTION

A Parade

CHARACTERS:

Cassander, Zerzabelle's Father
Zerzabelle, Cassander's Daughter
Leander, a Young Man in Love with Zerzabelle
Giles, Cassander's Valet

The action takes place in the street.

CASSANDER: (*Alone.*) I am alone. Let us take advantage of this auspicious soliloquy to summon my daughter and make a motion to her that she marry the husband of my choice, who will be personally selected for her by me as her destined spouse. I have not the slightest doubt of her assent, and if, by chance, she tried to use the pocket veto, I would give her one hundred swift kicks right in the stomach, which would constitute an assured plurality, and so, empowering the executive branch to act decisively, I shall now proceed to put her name in nomination. Zerzabelle! Zerzabelle!

(*Enter Zerzabelle.*)

ZERZABELLE: Here I am, father. I wasn't very far off. Since I saw that you were talking to yourself, and loud enough at that for the deaf to hear you, I drew close so as to listen, and that's how I learned that you plan to give me a husband and one hundred swift kicks right in the stomach. In response I have the honor of informing you, with my accustomed sweetness, that as for the husband, if he suits me I'll keep him, but as for the kicks, since they've never suited my stomach, I'll pay them back to you even before you've given them to me.

CASSANDER: Don't get so excited, daughter. It's true I spoke very loud, but I had my reasons for it and I must continue speaking in the same way, because the exposition isn't finished yet. My daughter, take a chair, so as to be more comfortably seated than if you remained standing, and listen carefully to what you already know. That will be the best way not to ignore what you have been acquainted with for a long long time.

ZERZABELLE: My dear father, your speeches are total nonsense; you get everything mixed up, but since I know that the duty of a submissive daughter is to obey, as long as it's not contrary to her wishes, I'm going to sit down.

CASSANDER: Now that will do, listen to me. I was born in the bosom of a respectable family, my parents neglected nothing to give me a first-rate education.

ZERZABELLE: But my dear father, you've told me a hundred times you never even knew who your father or mother was.

CASSANDER: Be quiet, daughter. I'll come back to that point later, but you've always got to begin a story exactly the way I did.

Well then, my parents gave me a first-rate education. I exceeded their fondest hopes and soon began to outstrip all my schoolmates.

ZERZABELLE: But, my father, you've never been able to read or write.

CASSANDER: Be quiet, will you. I'll come back to that later. Well then, soon I began to outstrip all my schoolmates. Next, I had to choose a profession: I selected a trade, which, as the saying goes, is the very soul of the Commercial Arts. I was born in the Faubourg Saint-Marceau; I might have lived and died there, but my predelictions carried me to far-off places of residence. So consequently I established a trading post on the banks of the Seine, near the Isle of Swans, and I devoted myself wholeheartedly to the manufacture of cheeses, intended for consumption by the worthy lower classes, whose enemies have never slandered them enough. My daughter, I have the impression that you've fallen asleep . . .

ZERZABELLE: (*Waking up.*) No, my father, I'm just getting ready to go to bed now . . .

CASSANDER: Stay, and listen to me: the worthy lower classes, whose enemies have never slandered them enough. Someone else in my place might well have cultivated his cheeses in America, but I did not want gold sullied by the blood of poor devils, who, simply for being no blacker than you are, my dear Zerzabelle, are no less your brothers.

ZERZABELLE: Is this story of yours going to last much longer?

CASSANDER: No doubt it will. You see, the important thing is for me to prove that I've always been a believer in democracy, even before the birth of the oldest members of the Chamber of Deputies. So then, I married your mother and you came into the world I know not how many months before our marriage.

ZERZABELLE: You always said it was two.

CASSANDER: I'll come back to that later. Your mother was taken from me by a pitiless fate, and from that point on I devoted myself to your upbringing. You amply rewarded my cares and became a phoenix.

ZERZABELLE: Oh, my father! The bowels of your compassion regard me with maternal indulgence. Phoenixes and I rarely keep company.

CASSANDER: No false modesty, my daughter. I know a thing or two about phoenixes and I assure you, you're one. But don't keep interrupting me. Entirely dedicated to the cares of your upbringing, I abandoned those of commerce to my valet Giles. I made him my first clerk, and so no one would challenge his title to the post, I employed no one other than him in my counting-house. I would even have made him my cashier, but I never kept any cash on hand. Because prudence always cautioned me to pocket the money I derived from the sale of my cheeses, instead of ever risking it in public funds, where it would have been exposed to the rapacity of various tontines, fraudulent bankruptcies, and other confidence tricks. My daughter, I thought I told you not to go to sleep.

ZERZABELLE: But, my father, it's impossible for me to stay awake when you tell those stories.

CASSANDER: Wait, it will soon be over. The Revolution ruined all of France's trade; the consumption of my cheeses went down from one day to the next. I came to the conclusion that the whole difficulty lay in the scarcity of floating funds. I proposed that the National Assembly issue a hundred million assignats, each worth six liards. My plan fell on deaf ears and I have therefore decided to turn over to Giles the entire business, since it no longer produces a decent dividend, and, at the same time, Giles will receive from me a still rarer, although less common, present: I shall give him in marriage the hand of my dear Zerzabelle.

ZERZABELLE: Gosh almighty! So, my father, that's where all that nonsense of yours was heading; you want me to become the wife of your valet Giles! Well, I'll tell you something, without any of all that high-falutin rigamarole: I shall never be the wife of your valet Giles. I only want to marry Mister Leander; he's the one I love and he's been my belover ever since I first set eyes on him.

CASSANDER: Oh, ho, you're adopting quite a demagogic tone now, my daughter. Who is this Leander of yours? Is he an aristocrat, or a democrat? Is he an active citizen?

ZERZABELLE: No, my father, I'm not adopting any decalogic tone. And Mister Leander is no Democritus or any Herostratus either. He's a very active Leander, and, what's more, he certainly must be a fine gentleman, because he carries a sword.

CASSANDER: What, wretched girl! You want to marry a nobleman? Oh putative daughter and degenerate foundling! If kicks were in the constitution, you'd receive them from me personally and that's all you'd ever get. But I have the feeling I'm wandering from the agenda. I declare the meeting adjourned, I abandon you to your aristocrat, and I disinherit you. (*He leaves.*)

ZERZABELLE: (*Alone.*) There, that's how the author of my days casts me off and sets me adrift. Why did I have to tell him about Mister Leander's birth, when I don't really know how it was done, or even if he was born at all. But here's Leander coming himself. Holy smoke, but does he ever look in a foul mood!

(*Enter Leander.*)

LEANDER: Oh, arms, heads! Death and destruction! Blood on the wall! Decrees and constitutions! A thousand kegs of powder and five hundred battalions! (*Swearing ferociously, Leander overturns all the furniture. Giles dashes in.*)

GILES: But who the devil are you so furious at, Mister Leander, that you're making such a row?

LEANDER: Oh! By one thousand squadrons of thirty-six pound cannon balls! If I only listened to the voice of my rage, I'd run my sword right through the whole National Assembly.

ZERZABELLE: But, my dear belover, what has the National Assembly done to you?

LEANDER: What has the National Assembly done to me? You'll soon find out, you vile plebeians! Listen to this! The National Assembly has forbidden anyone to put his coat of arms on the doors of his coach.

GILES: Well, what of it? That doesn't concern you, Mister Leander.

LEANDER: What do you mean, that doesn't concern me, infamous rabble? I suppose I don't have a coat of arms?

GILES: Maybe you do have a coat of arms, but you don't have a coach and so you don't have any coach doors.

LEANDER: Shut up, dregs of society. If I don't have a coach, it's only because I prefer open carriages which are lighter.

GILES: But you don't have an open carriage either.

LEANDER: If I don't have an open carriage, it's because they tip over too easily. Besides, it's none of your business, and I should like to inform you, commoners, that that's not all. The National Assembly has also decreed that no one will be permitted to put his coat of arms on the door of his town house.

GILES: Well, what of it, Mister Leander? Whatever the National Assembly has defleaed, it doesn't concern you either, since you don't have any town house.

LEANDER: I don't have any town house, insolent churl, because I live in the country. To tell the truth, since the city limits have been extended, my lands are now actually within Paris, but that won't keep me from having a town house, slob. And besides, that's not all! The National Assembly has outlawed the use of livery.

GILES: Oh! Well, how's that affect you? You don't have any servants.

LEANDER: Then you are not aware, you good-for-nothing, that my mother once used to have a servant. And if we did not require her to wear livery, it was because she served in our house as a lady's companion.

GILES: But, Mister Leander . . .

LEANDER: But, Mister smart aleck, I have put up with your impertinence quite long enough. I see that a counter-revolution is absolutely necessary, and I am going to start one here right now. At least I'll be able to say I've accomplished something. (*Leander begins thrashing Giles and throws him to the ground. Giles screams at the top of his lungs. Cassander arrives as a result of the noise.*)

CASSANDER: What's all this racket about?

GILES: (*On the ground.*) Oh, Sir, watch out! Mister Leander is starting a counter-revolution.

CASSANDER: A counter-revolution? I've arrived just in time to prevent it. Mister Leander, you must realize that . . .

LEANDER: What does that old halfwit want? (*He thrashes Cassander and tosses him on top of Giles; then he turns to Zerzabelle.*) Mamzelle, if it weren't for the code of chivalry I have sworn to uphold which renders the fair sex inviolable, I'd take care of you the same way I did those two scum.

CASSANDER: Whoever said there could be nothing worse than counter-revolution was absolutely right; now I can vouch for that by my own personal experience. Yet I have the means of preventing the counter-revolution from engulfing the entire country. This Leander is in love with my daughter. I'll offer him her hand in marriage, on the condition that henceforth he renounce all counter-revolutions. In this way, I'll have the opportunity to save France and be rewarded with a civic decoration. And I certainly won't fail to have that publicized in the newspapers. (*He gets up.*) Mister Leander?

LEANDER: What, Sir?

CASSANDER: Do you know, Sir, with whom you've just been speaking?

LEANDER: No, Sir. I only know that it was on your shoulders that I conveyed my message.

CASSANDER: Now then, Sir! These shoulders belong to Miss Zerzabelle's father.

LEANDER: Sir, I realized that Zerzabelle was a member of the bourgeoisie, and I am not at all surprised that I have thrashed the author of her days.

CASSANDER: You have only to say the word and you will have thrashed your own father-in-law. Because I am offering you an alliance with my family.

LEANDER: Sir, an alliance with your family is something that a nobleman wouldn't touch with a ten-foot pole, but the charms of your daughter resolve me to it and I consent to a misalliance.

CASSANDER: Do you promise never again to think of counter-revolution?

LEANDER: I promise, on the condition that you give me both Chambers, the Upper and the Lower.

CASSANDER: Counting the kitchen and the big alcove, that's just the number I've got in the house. But they're both on the same floor.

LEANDER: That will do, it's a bargain. And they told me it would be almost impossible to take both Chambers, and right away I got the two of them.

CASSANDER: Thanks to my spirit of conciliation, the counter-revolution has been averted.

LEANDER: Miss Zerzabelle, our happiness is assured, and we have only to apply ourselves to the embarrassment of riches that is your felicity.

GILES: Mister Leander, when you get the urge to start a counter-revolution, be so kind as to warn me, so I can be somewhere else.

LEANDER: Do not be afraid. Counter-revolution is no longer to be feared, since I have renounced it.

END

BIBLIOGRAPHY

The translation and introductory essay are based on the following sources.

Attinger, Gustave. *L'Esprit de la Commedia dell'Arte dans le théâtre français.* Paris: Librairie Théâtrale, 1950.

Beaumarchais. *Parades.* Ed. Pierre Larthomas. Paris: Société d'Édition d'Enseignement Superieur, 1977.

—. *Théâtre complet.* Ed. Maurice Allem and Paul-Courant. Paris: Bibliothèque de la Pléiade, 1957.

Beauvois, Daniel. "Introduction: Jean Potocki, Voyageur," in Jean Potocki, *Voyages en Turque et en Egypte, en Hollande, au Maroc,* ed. Daniel Beauvois. Paris: Fayard, 1980.

—. "Introduction: Du Cosmopolitisme à l'Imperialisme," in Jean Potocki, *Voyages dans les Steppes d'Astrakhan et du Caucase: Expédition en Chine,* ed. Daniel Beauvois. Paris: Fayard, 1980.

Bermel, Albert. *Farce.* New York: Simon & Schuster, 1982.

Brereton, Geoffrey. *French Comic Drama from the 16th to the 18th Century.* London: Methuen, 1977.

Brown, Frederick. *Theatre and Revolution: The Culture of the French Stage.* New York: Viking, 1980.

Caillois, Roger. "Préface," in Jean Potocki, *Manuscrit Trouvé à Saragosse.* Paris: Gallimard, 1958.

Crocker, Lester G. *The Age of Crisis: Man and World in Eighteenth-Century French Thought.* Baltimore: Johns Hopkins Press, 1959.

—, ed. *Diderot's Selected Writings.* Tr. Derek Coltman. New York: Macmillan, 1966.

Davis, Jessica Milner. *Farce.* London: Methuen, 1978.

Ducharte, Pierre Louis. *The Italian Comedy.* Tr. Randolph T. Weaver. New York: Dover, 1966.

Duchet, Michèle. *Anthropologie et Histoire au siècle des lumières.* Paris: Maspero, 1971.

Dzieduduszycka, Małgorzata. "New Productions: *The Dispute* by Henryk Tomaszewski," *Theatre in Poland,* 2 (246), 1979, 21-24.

Gueullette, J.-E. *Un Magistrat du XVIIIe siècle, ami des lettres, du théâtre et des plaisirs: Thomas-Simon Gueullette.* Paris: E. Droz, 1938.

Gueullette, Thomas-Simon. *Parades inédites.* Ed. and intro. Charles Gueullette. Paris: Librairie des Bibliophiles, 1885.

—. *Théâtre des Boulevards, ou recueil de parades*. A. Mahon, impr. Gilles Langlois, 1756, 3 vol.

Haskell, Francis. "Sad Clown: some notes on a 19th century myth," in *French 19th Century Painting*, ed. Ulrich Finke. New York: Harper & Row, 1972.

Hatzfeld, Helmut. *Literature through art; a new approach to French Literature.* Chapel Hill: University of North Carolina Press, 1969.

—. *The Rococo: Eroticism, Wit, and Elegance in European Literature.* New York: Pegasus, 1972.

Hauser, Arnold. *The Social History of Art*, III. New York: Vintage, 1958.

Hazard, Paul. *European Thought in the Eighteenth Century: From Montesquieu to Lessing.* New Haven: Yale University Press, 1954.

Huizinga, Johan. *Homo Ludens: a study of the play-element in culture.* Boston: Beacon Press, 1967.

Krakowski, Edouard. *Le comte Jean Potocki.* Paris: Gallimard, 1963.

Kowzan, Tadeusz. "La Parodie, le grotesque et l'absurde dans les *Parades* de Jean Potocki," (Actes du Colloque sur Jean Potocki, April, 1972) *Les Cahiers de Varsovie*, 3 (1975), 231-38.

Lamont, Rosette. "Patrice Chéreau: *La Dispute*," *Performing Arts Journal*, II, 1 (Spring 1977), 78-83.

Lintilhac, Eugène. *Beaumarchais et ses oeuvres.* Paris: Hachette, 1887.

McLendon, Will L. *Une ténébreuse carrière sous l'Empire et la Restauration: le Comte de Courchamps.* Paris: Minard, 1981.

Marivaux. *L'Île des Esclaves, La Colonie.* Ed. and intro. Jacqueline Cassalis. Paris: Larousse, 1969.

—. *Théâtre complet.* Ed. Marcel Arland. Paris: Bibliothèque de la Pléiade, 1949.

—. *Théâtre complet.* Ed. Frédéric Deloffre. Paris: Garnier, 1968, 2 vol.

Martin, Angus. "Présentation," in *Anthologie du Conte en France 1750-1799: Philosophes et coeurs sensibles.* Paris: Union Generale d'Éditions, 1981.

Mauzi, Robert. *L'Idée du bonheur dans la littérature et la pensée française au XVIIIe siècle.* Paris: Colin, 1960.

Miłosz, Czesław. *The History of Polish Literature.* New York: Macmillan, 1969.

Minguet, Philippe. *Esthétique du rococo.* Paris: J. Vrin, 1966.

Montesquieu. *The Persian Letters.* Tr. and ed. George R. Healy. Indianapolis: Bobbs-Merrill, 1964.

Moore, A.P. *The Genre Poissard and the French Stage of the Eighteenth Century.* New York: Publications of the Institute of French Studies, Inc., Columbia University, 1935.

Panofsky, Dora. "Gilles or Pierrot," *Gazette des Beaux Arts*, 39, 1952, pp. 319-40.

Picard, Raymond. *Two Centuries of French Literature.* Tr. John Cairncross. New York: McGraw-Hill, 1970.

Posner, Donald. *Watteau: A Lady at her Toilet.* New York: Viking, 1973.

Potocki, Jan. *Parady.* Tr. Józef Modrzejewski and intro. Leszek Kukulski. Warsaw: Czytelnik, 1966.

—. "Six Parades," intro. Roger Caillois, *Théâtre Populaire,* 34, 1959, pp. 51-79.

Proschwitz, Gunnar von. *Introduction à l'Étude du Vocabulaire de Beaumarchais.* (1956) Geneva: Slatkine Reprints, 1981.

Rousset, Jean. *Forme et Signification.* Paris: José Corti, 1963.

Schérer, Jacques. *Théâtre et anti-théâtre au XVIIIe siècle.* Oxford: Clarendon, 1975.

Sigaux, Gilbert. "Les *Parades* de Jean Potocki dans la Tradition du Théâtre de la Foire," (Actes du Colloque sur Jean Potocki, April, 1972) *Les Cahiers de Varsovie,* 3 (1975), 221-26.

Storey, Robert F. *Pierrot: A Critical History of a Mask.* Princeton, N.J.: Princeton University Press, 1978.

Sypher, Wylie. *From Rococo to Cubism in Art and Literature.* New York: Vintage, 1960.

Traz, Georges de (pseudonym François Fosca). *The Eighteenth Century: Watteau to Tiepolo.* Tr. Stuart Gilbert. Geneve: Skira, 1952.

Truchet, Jacques, ed. *Théâtre du XVIIIe Siecle,* I. Paris: Bibliothèque de la Pléiade, 1972.

Żółtowska, Maria Evelina. "Un Émule de Beaumarchais: Jean Potocki et ses *Parades.*" Paper delivered at the Canadian Society for Eighteenth-Century Studies, November 10, 1972.

PAJ PLAYSCRIPT SERIES

OTHER TITLES IN THE SERIES:

THEATRE OF THE RIDICULOUS/Kenneth Bernard, Charles Ludlam, Ronald Tavel

ANIMATIONS: A TRILOGY FOR MABOU MINES/Lee Breuer

THE RED ROBINS/Kenneth Koch

THE WOMEN'S PROJECT/Penelope Gilliatt, Lavonne Mueller, Rose Leiman Goldemberg, Joyce Aaron-Luna Tarlo, Kathleen Collins, Joan Schenkar, Phyllis Purscell

WORDPLAYS 1: NEW AMERICAN DRAMA/Maria Irene Fornes, Ronald Tavel, Jean-Claude van Itallie, Richard Nelson, William Hauptman, John Wellman

BEELZEBUB SONATA/Stanislaw I. Witkiewicz

DIVISION STREET AND OTHER PLAYS/Steve Tesich

TABLE SETTINGS/James Lapine

THE PRESIDENT AND EVE OF RETIREMENT/Thomas Bernhard

TWELVE DREAMS/James Lapine

COMEDY OF VANITY AND LIFE-TERMS/Elias Canetti

WORDPLAYS 2: NEW AMERICAN DRAMA/Rochelle Owens, Wallace Shawn, Len Jenkin, Harry Kondoleon, John O'Keefe

THE ENTHUSIASTS/Robert Musil

SICILIAN COMEDIES/Luigi Pirandello

RUSSIAN SATIRIC COMEDY/Babel, Krylov, Bulgakov, Ilf and Petrov, Evreinov, Prutkov

HAMLETMACHINE AND OTHER TEXTS FOR THE STAGE/Heiner Muller